The Only Way
FORWARD
is BACK

Jackson TerKeurst

With Kaley Rivera Thompson

The Only Way

FORWARD

is BACK

A Story of War, Adoption, and
Finding Your Purpose in God's Plan

150

YEARS STRONG

DAVID C COOK

THE ONLY WAY FORWARD IS BACK
Published by David C Cook
4050 Lee Vance Drive
Colorado Springs, CO 80918 U.S.A.

Integrity Music Limited, a Division of David C Cook
Brighton, East Sussex BN1 2RE, England

DAVID C COOK®, the graphic circle C logo and related marks
are registered trademarks of David C Cook.

Library of Congress Control Number 2024943980
ISBN 978-0-8307-8793-7
eISBN 978-0-8307-8794-4

© 2025 Jackson TerKeurst

The Team: Luke McKinnon, Julie Cantrell, Stephanie Bennett, Judy
Gillispie, Leigh Davidson, James Hershberger, Karen Sherry
Grooming: Marz Collins
Cover Design: Brian Mellema
Cover Photo: Robby Klein

Printed in the United States of America
First Edition 2025

1 2 3 4 5 6 7 8 9 10

040725

To Amanda, my greatest inspiration.
And Legend and Londyn, my
greatest joys and blessings.

CONTENTS

INTRODUCTION

Who am I?

To know who we are, we have to start with who we were.

So let's start here.

I was the ...

Grandson of a witch doctor.

The son of a town chief.

A Liberian orphan.

A statistic of war.

Nameless.

Homeless.

Barely alive.

But I'm none of those things now. In my thirties, I'm blessed, safe, and finally able to dig my feet into the American soil where God has planted me. However, I have a nagging longing to revisit my story. Memories keep rising up from the African dirt that has settled in the corners of my mind. I must dust these memories off, hold them out to you, and let you see how God can truly bring life from death, give the abandoned a home, favor the lowly, offer second chances, and provide for our most basic needs even in incredible poverty.

For me, **the only way forward is back**.

I hope in the process of telling the story of where I've been that you may uncover some of your own story along the way. By examining where *we* have been, it will become clear who God has been preparing *us* to be.

While you may have not lived through the Liberian Civil War, you're fighting your own battles and witnessing your own carnage. Maybe you too have been abandoned or orphaned. Possibly, you're considering a mission trip to Liberia or a neighboring African country. Praise God if you are thinking about adopting!

Yes, this book is about the life of Jackson TerKeurst, but it's also about you and the God who is for us all.

As you read, may you discover God's hand in every chapter of your story and see Him preparing to scribe something beautiful in the unwritten pages.

So, who am I?

Who are you?

Who will we be?

If you're ready to move forward, let's go back …

Section 1

FOBLITE IS ON FIRE

A deer thirsts for a stream of water.
In the same way, I thirst for you, God.
I thirst for the living God.
When can I go to meet with him?
Day and night, my tears have been my food.
People are always saying,
"Where is your God?"
When I remember these things ...

Psalm 42:1–4 (ICB)

What comes to your mind when you think of the word *corruption*? For me, it triggers a thousand memories and sounds—this one in particular ...

In the black of midnight, I'm seven years old when I'm awakened by the blinding flash of an explosion followed by leaping flames. Outside, I spot men who must be rebel soldiers trying to infiltrate my village. Their unity as a group but random dress lets me know that they are not part of the Liberian army but one of the many rogue rebel groups fighting to take power during our government's downfall. Men and young children (even younger than me) are running with guns in hand as huts burn to the ground. The smell of gasoline fills my nose, and smoke clouds my vision as the sounds of war erupt around me. Guns firing. Bombs exploding. Women screaming for their children, who yell back in terror. I cover my ears, trying to block the awful cries of girls being raped, of bodies being chopped with machetes.

Flames from nearby huts light our family's shared bedroom. On any normal night, I would find my mother and brother sleeping soundly on the beds near me. But now, I'm the only one here in the house.

What is happening? Where is my mom? Does she have my brother? Why did they leave me? I'm only a kid; what should I do?

Suddenly, my heart begins to race, my hands become sticky, and sweat pours from my forehead. Breathing heavily, I drop off my bamboo bed onto our dirt floor.

Like a soldier creeping through the brush, I crawl flat on my belly until I reach the back of the hut. Within seconds, rebels are pounding on the wooden door, trying to knock it down. A gurgling sound comes from high above me outside as rebels pour gasoline over our scrap metal roof. I'm still inside when my home bursts into flames.

From out of nowhere, my mom's sister, Auntie* Kemah, grabs me by the hand. She lives with us in our hut but didn't seem to be here just a second ago when my dreaming shattered into a living nightmare. *Where did she come from?* Without a word, she throws me onto her back, and we barely escape into the safety of the thick brush that surrounds our village. Thorns tear our bodies as we rush into the dense jungle, but I don't care. I feel nothing. Surviving is all my brain can think about. Living is the only thing that matters.

For a moment, I look back. Turning for a final view of my village, Foblite, I watch in horror as fire engulfs every structure, flames swallowing my entire world.

My neighbor rushes toward us. He's headed to join us in our jungle haven when his eyes grow big and white, and he falls to the ground. He's been shot in the back while fleeing for his life. I have no time to process the horrors playing out around me. These images sear into my mind as I take my last glimpse of home, turn toward my auntie, and sink back toward the jungle. Our eyes say what our words can't, and our bodies obey. *Run!*

Listen, I know this is a hard place to start a book. We like the comfort that comes from reading something soft and inspirational. Part of my story may offer some of this. But I have to start with this traumatic childhood scene because it's in the chaos that God taught (and continues to teach) me the value of human life and community.

This attack happened in the early nineties, catching me in the crossfires of Africa's bloodiest civil war.[1] The lives of more than 250,000 Liberians were taken, and a million others were displaced in refugee camps in neighboring countries.[2]

They say that history repeats itself. I hope you'll take the next section to heart so it doesn't.

A Quick History

I'm not here to write a history book, and you probably didn't buy this book to read one. I'm glad we're on the same page here. However, there are a few things you need to know to fully understand this story. So I'll keep this as short and to the point as possible and make my best effort to not sound like the teacher in Charlie Brown.

Here we go …

Liberia was formed into a democracy in the mid-1800s when Americans attempted to return freed slaves back to the continent from which they had been taken. However, these were second- or third-generation African Americans who had never actually set foot on African soil. Nevertheless, the American Colonization Society sent state legislatures and colonial agent Eli Ayers to the Pepper Coast aboard a US Navy ship commanded by Lieutenant Robert F. Stockton. The two men approached the leader of the Gola people, a native tribe residing in the area, and purchased Cape Mesurado to place the first settlement of eighty-six Black volunteers and a smaller group of missionaries.

In total, five other settlements came to Cape Mesurado over the years. They struggled greatly from poor crop growth, disease, tribal attacks from outside groups, and lack of support from the American Colonization Society and American federal government. Despite the odds, these settlements took root and grew into a city they called "Monrovia," named after US President Monroe. They even formed a functioning government modeled after their American counterpart and elected their first Black governor, Joseph Jenkins Roberts, in 1842. Due to its large production of natural rubber and Monrovia's ability to serve as a port city, Liberia became a fairly successful country. At least, it appeared so to the outside world.

Through the early to mid-1900s, Liberia continued to hold elections and expand the government's power. However, it's important to understand that, by this time, the country was trying to please two distinct groups of people: the native people, who functioned under their tribal law, and America-Liberians, who were former slaves that had been brought to Liberia from America and were running the country under a democratic oligarchy. Between these two groups of Liberians, significant corruption, tribal angst, and racial tension had long been brewing.

In 1971, when William R. Tolbert took office as the president of Liberia, threats from outside tribes and organized groups started to shake the democratic foundation of the new country. Grassroots movements began to rise outside the city and, without any real power to put elected officials in office, some protestors began to throw around the idea of a coup, a total overthrow of the government using mass brutality. A group of seventeen uneducated Liberian soldiers had united under the leadership of former soldier Thomas Quiwonkpa and senior member Master Sergeant Samuel Doe to put this violent idea into action.

Late at night on April 12, 1980, Quiwonkpa and his colleagues entered the Liberian presidential palace and brutally murdered Tolbert and any officers or officials inside. In one swoop, they wiped out the America-Liberian oligarchy that had been governing the country for more than a century.

The next morning, these rebels ran the following message across all scheduled programming:

> I am Master Sergeant Samuel K. Doe. I have killed President Tolbert and we have taken control of the government. All soldiers report to Barclay Training Center. Do not take orders from your officers. All military officers stay in your homes. If you go out, you will be shot. Members of the Tolbert Administration, turn yourselves in to the Post Stockade. People of Liberia stay off the streets. We have won. In the cause of the people the struggle continues.[3]

This last line would become the tagline used by Doe, who had now assumed leadership, and his men, who quickly formed what was known as the "People's Redemption Council" or PRC.

Doe and the PRC quickly took full power and, with it, the interest of a thirty-two-year-old Liberian who had been educated as an economics student in America, Charles Taylor. While Taylor was not directly involved in the coup, he did support their mission to give dominion back to native people and wipe out the current governing system. He saw a blank slate for Liberia as an opportunity to gain authority and control, so when the PRC came to power, Taylor was elected to office as Director General of the General Services Agency.[4]

Several key players and officers impacted this rebellion, but Taylor is the main man we need to focus on for the purpose of my story. His actions were the match that set off the fireworks of Liberia's civil war.

As the child of an indigenous Liberian mother and Americo-Liberian father, Taylor was well educated and known for being able to blend in, sway officials, and talk his way into almost every room. By all reports, he was strategic and made all the right connections. In just ten years, Taylor gained ground in this new government, eluded jail, started to build an army, and decided to make a full climb to power.[5]

On December 24, 1989, nearly a decade after Doe had killed President Tolbert, the British Broadcasting Corporation (BBC) newsroom telephone rang. The caller stated his name was Charles Taylor. He wanted to announce his invasion of Liberia and intention to take Samuel Doe from power.

The news team pulled together a quick interview with Taylor and broadcast the takeover of Liberia to the world.[6]

Around this same time, as warlords began emerging and Taylor's rebel army groups started to terrorize and pillage villages, I was born. Some of my earliest memories are of destruction.

It only takes a quick Google search on the Liberian Civil War to see images of child soldiers weighted down by bullets and guns. If you scroll through, you'll witness even more pictures of carnage, fighting, death, and destruction. They don't call it "Africa's bloodiest civil war" for nothing. How I didn't end up in the dead center of this as a child soldier myself, I'm not sure. My only explanation is that God must have had His hand directly on me. Now that you know the historical events that forced me, as a seven-year-old boy, to flee to the jungle that night as my village was burned and my neighbors were killed, let's jump back into my story.

Home Away from Home

Auntie Kemah and I have been running through the dense, green jungle for hours on end. The thick canopy of palm and evergreen trees blocks out most of the stars, and I'm certain this is the darkest night of my life. By the time we finally collapse, too exhausted to continue, the trauma takes over my tiny body. I'm shivering uncontrollably and fighting waves of nausea. *What did I just see? Was that even real? Where am I?*

Shaking nearly as much as me, Kemah gathers me up in her arms and holds me tight, as if her hug could reattach the childhood innocence and peace that was just brutally torn from me. I wish she could squeeze the scenes of death and violence from my mind, but no matter how comforting her embrace might feel, she can't change our harsh new reality. The only thing that keeps me breathing is knowing I am not alone. By no small miracle, we still have each other.

As she holds me close, my breathing calms and the panic that's been coursing through my body turns into a settled awareness. I inhale to fill my lungs with the humid air. The rich smell of rain and earth steams from the thick, lush vegetation. All around us, drops of water roll off the tops of the towering palm and fruit trees. Animals and insects call from their hiding places, their chorus underscored by the gurgle of a nearby stream. We are now one of these living, hidden things, tucked away from all signs of people, deep, deep in the jungle. Far too deep to find a way back out. With only the clothes on our backs, we are lost refugees in desperate need of shelter.

Judging by the way the sun is peeking its dimming light through the jungle's canopy, Foblite must have been attacked in the early hours, around three or four in the morning. We've been on the run now for almost a full day, and it will be dark again in just a few hours. Auntie Kemah follows my line of sight and seems to notice this too. She beckons me with a wave of her hand and nods for us to keep going. We've created our own form of sign language because we're too afraid to speak.

We draw even further back into the jungle where we can remain completely hidden. Like a little oasis, we find a space near a stream of water with mangos and bananas growing nearby. Perfect. Using our bare hands, we break off a few tree limbs and begin to construct our new home away from home.

Banana House

Have you ever constructed a banana house? What!? You haven't?

I'm kidding. It's not a normal thing to do. However, Liberians are resourceful. Anyone can create something from nothing when they are desperate. And we were indeed desperate.

When you're in survival mode, you begin to run a mental checklist to secure your most basic needs. Here's how mine went:

Food, check.

Drink, check.

Next on the list—shelter.

No matter where you are, you have to have shelter to survive. But this is especially true in the jungle. As we quickly scan our surroundings for building supplies, we point out banana trees, palm trees, bamboo, and rooted ropes.* Judging by our supply list, I know it is my time to shine.

Every now and again, a bad habit can be used for good, and this becomes one of those moments. Clearly aware of my mischievous reputation for climbing high trees with my brother, Auntie Kemah makes an exception to the "no climbing trees" rule and, with a nod of her head, she motions for me to climb one of the rainforest's young trees and hang on the end of the limb.

The tree is perfect for a young boy—not so big that I can't wrap my arms around the trunk but not so small it can't support my weight. Using just my arms and legs, I quickly shimmy up and over the trunk until I reach the top. Then, I swing my weight like a monkey to bend the narrow body of the tree low enough for Auntie to break off the branches we need. Jumping back to the ground, I release the tree and it whips back upright to reveal only a few gaps as evidence of the limbs we stole.

---

* For definitions of Liberian terms and concepts, marked throughout the book with asterisks, please see the Liberian Dictionary in the appendix.

This works! Genius.

Next, we collect several bamboo stalks and tie them together in the shape of a bed frame using long tree roots as ropes to keep it intact. We discover a patch of banana trees nearby, and that provides enough large leaves for us to put together a roof for our new, makeshift hut.

We also grab a few palm tree branches and set them around for privacy, shade, and protection. As a finishing touch, we place a banana leaf on the bamboo bed we created. We're both hoping it will provide some ease to our bodies despite the discomfort of a hard tree bed.

Our final to-do is to tilt the roof in the right direction for water to run off. The only thing worse than a hard tree bed is a hard tree bed full of water.

When we finish, like artists after painting their final brushstrokes, we both take a breath and step back to examine our best efforts.

I can't believe it. We did it.

Boom! Banana House.

There is no exhaustion like the kind that follows running for your life and then constructing a house in the jungle with nothing but your own hands. I'm tired to the bone, but I'm having trouble falling to sleep tonight. I'm overwhelmingly thankful for Banana House and Auntie Kemah because, here in our little jungle hideout, we are safe … for now, at least.

Despite finding some reprieve, I'm still just a kid who, less than a day ago, witnessed a war and was ripped from my family. I deeply miss them. Are they even alive? I picture their faces, my most recent memories with them, and tears flow down my face in a quiet, constant stream. I lay on the banana bed in the depth of the dark jungle, longing to play with my younger brother, my best friend. But he is nowhere to be found.

Silent in the Chaos

The war taught me how fragile life is. I feared for my soul every second. Hiding in that jungle, I would panic anytime I heard the slightest sound of a limb falling from a tree or the footsteps of an animal. To hide, I'd push myself even deeper into the brush in case any noise signaled a rebel soldier's arrival.

I began to live by three important rules:

1. Keep your ears sharp.
2. Leave your eyes wide open.
3. Stay quiet.

I even trained myself not to cough, sneeze, or even think about crying. My muscles memorized how to remain still and quiet. Auntie Kemah and I barely talked above a whisper for months, and we both kept our eyes and ears wide open.

Of course, being silent in the chaos is exactly where Satan wants all of us to be.

Like a master magician, Satan uses chaos to manipulate our attention. In the Bible, the book of John calls him "the father of lies" (John 8:44). We become so bought into the enemy's scheme that we don't notice the trick that's actually occurring. Now you see it. Now you don't.

> **Being silent in the chaos is exactly where Satan wants all of us to be.** »»»

Chaos distracts us, while the Devil destroys. At first, too afraid to come out of hiding, my auntie and I stayed silent in the chaos, which is exactly what Satan wanted us to do.

The Road to Joe Town

After several months of hiding in the jungle, Auntie Kemah and I become desperate for support, food, and better shelter. She suggests we travel to Joe Town, where my dad lives. Possibly, they haven't been attacked. If we're going to survive and not starve out here in the jungle, we don't have much of a choice. "Okay, let's go," I whisper.

We load up a meager supply of food and begin the long walk. The journey seems endless, but I trust my auntie's sense of direction. We come from a long line of farmers, so she knows the lay of the land.

After more than six hours have passed, we've covered at least twelve miles. I remember and follow my three rules. *Keep your ears sharp. Leave your eyes wide open. Stay quiet.* To stay alive, we pay attention to every sound. As we draw closer to Joe Town, our senses become even sharper. If we hear a truck, we hide. It's rebels for sure. People traveling by foot could be villagers, but they could also be soldiers looking for their next kill. There's no way to know for sure, so we hide from everyone.

At some point, we finally feel safe enough to walk on the road, so we travel by that easier path until it turns into one of the hardest obstacles we have yet to overcome.

We're already upon the bridge by the time we spot the military checkpoint. I know government soldiers aren't rebels, which calms my spirit just a little. However, these "officials" can be just as evil and corrupt. My heart rate quickens, and my stomach lurches into my throat as two soldiers stroll over to us and immediately search our bodies for guns and weapons.

"Blow air into your mouth," we're commanded.

What? I dare not ask why. The look on Auntie Kemah's face says, "Just do it." We both know the consequence of disobedience is death, so we lower our eyes, awkwardly close our mouths, and balloon our cheeks out with air. For a moment nothing happens, and we just keep standing there in front of the soldiers, humiliated because we look like wild animals storing away food in our cheeks.

The soldiers smack our faces, simply for entertainment. We are a joke to them. Nothing more. So they let us through the checkpoint, and we proceed across the bridge.

Whew, thank God. That was close.

As the soldiers shuffle us forward, we continue down the road. But we're only a few steps into our journey when commotion erupts behind us. Soldiers grab a man just a few feet from me and take him behind the checkpoint we were just standing in front of. Without warning, a loud *POW!* of gunfire fills the air.

They killed him? They killed him!

My gut churns and my head spins, but I dare not look back. *Why was he shot? Was he suspicious? How did we make it through and he didn't? Why not us, God?* Thoughts flood my mind, but I don't have time to process any of them. My legs become as heavy as bags of grain, but we have to move forward or we'll be next.

"Go! Go! Move!" The soldiers shout, hitting us in the backs with their guns.

It takes all the willpower I have to fight the natural instinct to run for my life. I know that if we move too quickly, they will shoot us. So we walk as fast as our legs will carry us, careful to keep our heads down as we keep moving toward Joe Town. Dead bodies litter the streets, and I try not to look at them, feeling both sad for the victims and grateful that I am not one of them. In the distance, a truck rumbles down the road, so we jump back into the bush to hide. It's safer if we stay out of sight, so we'll be taking the back roads from here all the way to my dad's village.

Joe Town

Upon arrival, our hopes are dashed. Rebel soldiers have already reached Joe Town. However, they don't officially "occupy" the village yet. So Auntie Kemah and I dare to enter the village in hopes of finding our family. With not knowing the fate of my mother or other relatives from Foblite, sheer relief washes over me as I discover that my half brothers, half sisters, and father are safe in Joe Town, as well as all my paternal aunties. When we embrace one another, I let out a breath I didn't know I'd been holding for months now. Muscles relax that I didn't know had been tense.

I finally pause long enough to notice the sky. My parents were never married, so I grew up with my mom and her children (my other half brothers and sisters) in Foblite. Sadly, the sky here in Joe Town is not putting on the West African evening show I am used to watching. Where the sun usually casts brilliant orange and pink hues across an endless horizon before being tucked in by a brilliant blanket of stars, this evening the sky appears ash gray and blood red, colors I've never seen in a Liberian sunset. I don't know what this means. Is this a good or bad omen? Are that many villages and bodies on fire? Or has even the sun grown weary of all the destruction it has seen as it hovers over our devastated country?

Despite the falling sky, there is a sense of home here, and I let that sink in. The God behind the discolored sunset whispers to me that this suffering may be short-lived. He tells me, "Live this moment. Be a child. Be alive."

So that's what I try to do.

My friends and I escape the war for a moment to play a traditional Liberian game called Lappa.* We divide into two teams and toss all our shoes into one large pile. One player jumps into the middle of the pile and tries to organize the shoes without getting hit by the ganga ball,* which is made of rubber (from a rubber tree) and wrapped in old socks.

I laugh and run, thinking about what else we may play. Tire? Wheel? Maybe a game of Nails War? For the moment, we are ordinary Liberian kids and we're having a blast!

But then, a truck pulls up in the village. And just like that we're yanked out of our play world and back into the war.

Our game halts immediately as our parents scream out for us. "Come here! Hurry!"

We race toward our huts, and I know full well the terror that is coming. Time again stands still as the adrenaline of running for my life shoots like fire back into my veins. I'm familiar now with the sheer need to survive and what the body does in panic mode. I let the fear fuel me with the energy I need to flee.

"Grab your siblings and run to the woods," my dad commands my older brother. "Now!"

I'm reliving the attack in Foblite, my mom's village, as my siblings and I race toward the woods. There, we hide.

We don't go too far because we want to see what will happen. It might seem strange to hang around when your life is in jeopardy, but there is some peace in witnessing the truth of an experience—even the most traumatic moments in our lives. I know the torture of trying to imagine what might have happened to the people you love, people who were stripped from you in war. I know the pain of never finding answers to the questions: Were they brutally killed? Are they prisoners? Are they slaves? Did they somehow survive and are hiding in the woods, maybe not far from us?

The questions are endless, especially when you're a child and your brain is still able to invent boundless options. It's better to risk staying close by so we can know for sure. All the adults have to stay behind, and we children need to know how this turns out for them. That way we don't dream up the worst. We'll just know it, and then we'll have to find a way to accept it.

I peek up from the bush when I hear a loud *BAP!* It's the sound of flesh and bone colliding. I watch as my dad takes a hard punch in the gut from a rebel soldier.

"Who's the man here? Who's in charge?" they ask.

The answer, of course, is my dad, the chief. But no one dares speak his name. No one replies at all, so the beatings continue until the men are weak enough for the soldiers to force them into their truck.

After most of them are loaded, including my father, the soldiers move toward the back of the vehicle and open the trunk. Several dead bodies roll out to the ground. I'm stunned as the soldiers begin to cut open the cadavers, pull out their guts, and cut off their heads. In my short life, I've seen terrible things, but this tops the list as the most gruesome I've ever witnessed. It takes everything I have to hold back the bile rising in my throat.

We keep watching as the rebels begin to set up a checkpoint with a gate, blocking off the only entry to Joe Town (and the villages that lie beyond it). They place two posts, one on each side of the road, and set a human head on the top of each. Then they drape the intestines of the bodies across the gate as the checkpoint rope. This isn't only a blockade; it's a warning sign.

"You should eat a baby, man!" I hear one of the rebels tell his companion. "It will make you strong!" He goes on to brag about baby killing while other men in the group fire their guns up into the air for fun. These are not men; these are monsters. They are scarier than anything my childhood imagination ever dreamed might lurk in the forest. Maybe they are the Devil himself.

The truck pulls away, taking my dad, my uncle, and other prisoners off to what I can only assume will be their brutal deaths. Both of my parents and most of my family are now gone.

I'm hit now with a harsh reality that no kid ever wants to face.

Who am I?

I have no parents.

I am an orphan.

But I keep moving forward.

Destroying the Devil

If these early memories taught me anything, it's that God is working amid and against chaos. First John 3:8 states, "The one who does what is sinful is of the devil, because the devil has been sinning from the beginning. The reason the Son of God appeared was to destroy the devil's work."

While the Devil is trying to destroy us, God is actually destroying him. Mostly, God is doing this through community.

Have you ever noticed how chaos draws people together like magnets? Despite the war growing around us, life in my village before we were raided was peaceful. We all knew each other by name, and families were close. Every night, we would all gather in the center of the village with chairs, palm wine, drums, and sasa* and sing the night away. The children would run, laugh, and play tag.

> **Being with people puts back together what has been broken.**

Some nights, we sat with our legs crossed in the dirt, hands tucked under our chins. The firelight cast dancing shadows across our young, curious faces as we leaned forward to take in every word of the storyteller sharing an ancient tale about our ancestors. Afterward, we would scatter off into small groups, taking turns to tell an animated story of our own.

Yes, community is the remedy for chaos. Being with people puts back together what has been broken. But even when we can't count on others, there is a God who promises to never leave (Deut. 31:8).

In the middle of the war, when I zeroed in on the chaos (as we all do), I lost sight of God. I cried out for Him to rescue me, my family, and my country from the hands of evil. *Why was there so much killing and destruction? Where was God?*

In hindsight, everything is twenty-twenty, right? Now, I see so clearly that God was there protecting me every step of the way.

God can use chaos to start a new chapter in our lives and draw us into a more connected community. How do I know? Just watch what happens next!

Section 2

TRUSTING GOD IN ABANDONMENT

Arms in the hands of children ...
Machine gun lyricists singing the blood
soaked hymns of the dispossessed.

Jeremy Dehart, "Civil War in Liberia"

I'm terrified.

I was separated from Auntie Kemah in the attack at Joe Town. I'm still trying to let it sink in that both my parents are probably dead, that I'm now an orphan at seven years of age, but there's not even a moment of peace to process this harsh new reality.

My paternal half brother Jerry, two older half sisters, and I escaped their home in Joe Town and are now en route through the woods to a neighboring town of Gbarnga.* We hope to meet my dad's brother at our family's house. It's the only place we know to go. Some children and a few adults managed to escape with us, so we're all headed in the same direction—toward an unknown future.

We're as silent as possible as we all travel through the jungle. That's why it's ear piercing when shots from an AK-47 ring out through the canopy of trees above our heads. We are already spooked, our nerves frayed from what we just witnessed at Joe Town, so the sound of the shots are like the crack of a starting pistol signaling the beginning of the race for our lives. We are no longer rational people thinking of maintaining safety in our group. We are now animals, and it's every living being for themselves. We have become prey, diving for cover in all directions as the predators fire their guns from an army truck.

I latch on to anyone close to me and follow the other boys and girls my age who dive under thick brush. We are now a pack of children crawling on our forearms and bellies, doing our best to not be shot while still heading toward my uncle's house.

We crawl forever. Only when the gunfire becomes a distant echo does the shuffle of our bodies, crunching of the brush, and hard breathing start to slow. We are at the edge of the jungle by the time I realize something terrible.

My brother and sisters are not with me anymore.
I have now lost my siblings.
Everyone. Everyone in my family is gone.

———

I am lonely but not lost. Now alone, I walk in the woods several days toward Gbarnga until I come across a familiar village. I know I'm near my uncle's town, so my hopes soar at the thought that we may find other survivors and receive some help.

As I walk into the village, I'm hit with a terrible smell, like when a mouse has died in the wall of your hut and you don't find its body until days later. But this is worse. Much worse.

Making my way into the town, my hopes collapse. Dead bodies lie scattered across the ground. Judging by the maggots that crawl in and out of the cadavers, the attack here must have happened days ago. I'm still just seven years old, and I hate that I now know how to calculate how long a person has been dead based on the look of their body breaking down and becoming, once again, African dirt.

I hold my nose as I quietly sneak around the village. It doesn't look like any military personnel hung around after this raid, but I can't be too careful. I didn't come this far just to bump into a soldier and die here.

I run between the mud houses with my nose pinched until I finally reach Gbarnga. *There's our family's home! And, I can't believe it, there's my uncle!*

"Cammué!* There you are!" he shouts.

Here I am! Yes, somehow, I am still here.

How have I survived? Will I ever see my parents again? My siblings? Will the rebels ever release my father? I'm a kid with a million questions, but I have no answers or security in sight. There is nothing, I mean nothing, worse than this.

In Gbarnga, our family house is located right next to one of the biggest churches in the city. Just a few miles from there lies an abandoned elementary school building that is now being used as an orphanage called Mother Davis's orphanage. A town Mother,* Miss Evelyn, has started to take kids off the streets, hoping to keep them safe from rebel recruiters who are forcing orphans like me into joining their war as child soldiers.

With our family so scattered, I'm relieved to have found my uncle, and I plan to stay here with him. But then he tells me the words I don't want to hear. "Cammué, I'm going to take you to a place that is safer than being with me," he explains. "When the war is over, I will find your mother and father and tell them to come get you."

I plead with him not to take me to Mother Davis's orphanage. I sob through my pleas, explaining that I just want to go back to the farm and find my mom. But even my most sincere begging is no use. We both know what we don't want to admit. Both of my parents are probably dead, and my uncle is not able to protect me. As an orphan, I belong at an orphanage now.

It's time to leave. I hold on tight as my uncle takes me by the hand, and we embark on foot to the orphanage in Gbarnga. First, we walk up a long hill that crests over a big open field full of burning trash. I take very shallow breaths, trying not to inhale the stench, until we reach a swampy area where we carefully trek through to reach the other side of town. Here, tall stalks of sugar cane line the road where more trash, debris, and old vehicles have been abandoned.

We round the corner to find vendors selling local Liberian fare from their farms. People are buying and trading, as they were during my previous visits to this market, but things are different now. Half the vendor stands have been burned to the ground. Other booths escaped with the war wounds of charred corners and smoked edges.

My eyes search the market as we walk, as if my mom or dad might appear at any moment and we could run away together far from this orphanage. Even though my mind knows they are not here and may not even be alive, it takes a minute for my heart to catch up. Finally, my hopes too become ash as we pass the market—vacant of anyone who will let me run away with them—and arrive at the orphanage.

The orphanage in Gbarnga consists of a bunch of run-down buildings awkwardly cemented together, attempting to appear like it's in one piece. It looks exactly how my fragmented soul feels. As I wave goodbye to my uncle, I too am attempting to appear like my heart is in one piece, like I'm not the shell of the child I once was. I tuck my only belongings—a meager pair of pants and shirt I carry in a plastic bag—under my arms and squeeze them as if I can wring comfort from the wrinkle of plastic and ware of cloth.

This is not the embrace I need. I need my mother, my brother. It's been months since I've seen any of my immediate family members. Tears well in my eyes as the thought of them all dead appears like another unwanted, unpredicted attack.

Again, I'm panicking. *Breathe.* I squeeze the bag tighter and hold on for dear life to the only things that haven't left me yet. *God, protect my family members. Send them to come get me from this place,* I silently pray.

I'm handed to a woman named Miss Evelyn, but all I notice is the overwhelming smell of feces and the piles of trash in all directions. As I walk through the building, it's clear there's no sanitation and everyone throws garbage into piles around the orphanage. The facility is now home to hundreds of kids like me, some injured from the war. Most of the children appear to be malnourished, leaning against the side of the building as if they are just waiting their turn to die. Now, I am one of them.

Is that what we're all doing here, waiting our turn to die?

My eyes turn away from the devastation and toward Miss Evelyn, the head of the facility. I am relieved to learn that she's from the Kpelle tribe, the same as me. Tribe is close to family, and I take whatever comfort I can from that bond. A tiny flame of hope stirs from the ashes, and I cling to its light in this darkness with all my might.

After a while, I fall into a normal routine (whatever "normal" means for starving orphans who are just barely getting by). Our breakfast typically consists of cornmeal, sugar, and canned milk (similar to Boost). We attend school lessons and learn our Kpelle alphabet. With whatever energy we can muster up, we play.

No food is available for days at a time. I become so lightheaded that I can't stand up on my own two feet. Maybe again today I will lie on the ground until God gives me the strength I need to make my way to the dump pile and scrounge up something to eat.

My thoughts of a dump-pile dinner are interrupted when I see soldiers pulling up to the orphanage. I'm worried about what might happen, but I no longer have the energy to care. I stare at them, lifeless as a skeleton, almost hoping they will put me out of my misery once and for all. But then I realize they are unloading bags of rice. I overhear them tell our leaders that Charles Taylor, the rebel ringleader who resided in Gbarnga at that time, was informed of our situation and decided to send aid. *Are we in such terrible shape that even the evilest man alive has compassion for us orphans?* The way my bones protrude from under my thin skin tells me maybe so.

Like Job in the Bible, I think about how God loved him and his family yet gave the Devil permission to test him. In response, the Devil stripped Job of his family, belongings, home, everything. Despite all the trials and tribulations Job faced, he kept his eyes on God and sought Him out. So God returned to Job everything Satan had stolen and gave him double the amount he once owned. I decide to do the same and hope God will eventually decide to bless me too. Maybe instead of one serving of rice, God will give me two for my troubles.

There is food. For now, we survive.

Attack at Gbarnga

Most kids are afraid of monsters under their beds or things that go "bump" in the night. Their nightmares are of fictional ghosts that will never actually visit them, much less harm them. When you're a child in a war, your nightmares are filled with memories of death, violence, gunfire, and darkness. You live your waking hours knowing your darkest dreams could become reality at any moment. You're living in hell, and there is no waking to escape.

It's around midday, and I'm working with other children on learning letters. We're all so much better with food in our bellies. My brain actually works again. I can remember things! We have energy to play and laugh even. *Let's see, what letter comes next ...*

But then my train of thought is interrupted by a sound that will forever be etched into my memory. Around the classroom, we're all stunned by the loud explosion. My muscles tense as I fight the urge to run. Every kid in this place reverts back to the survival instincts we've all learned. Using our innate senses is the only way we've made it this far.

My eyes close as déjà vu sinks in. I'm back in my home village of Foblite, women are screaming, bombs are going off. Death is everywhere. I open my eyes and feel my gut lurch as I let the recognition of that sound sink in. It's a grenade launcher, and once again the noises from our collective nightmares become reality.

Within minutes, the eardrum-shattering sounds of AK-47 gunfire fills the air. Now is the time for my body to move.

I run as fast as I can to a corner in the classroom that seems protected from the flying bullets. Everyone is screaming, crying, panicking, and fearing for our lives. We have all experienced this war before, and yet, not even familiarity can numb the sheer terror we all feel inside.

"Everyone, lay down on the floor! Do not look up or move," our caregiver screams. She hasn't even finished giving us her warning before bullets fly through the windows. We hold our breath and throw up prayers, hoping one of our pleas hits God like the bullet shells bouncing off the walls of our classroom. Peeping through a crack in the wall, I see rebels spreading throughout the orphanage grounds, forcefully dragging young girls across the dirt, tearing at their clothes and bodies.

"Mom! Dad! Save me," I cry in vain. I have no family, no one to hear. No one to care. In a room full of people, I am alone.

No one is safe.

There is a break in the attack. The rebels have apparently finished storming the compound, recruiting children for soldiers, and molesting the girls. They had been hanging around the compound for a few hours, but now we don't see any more soldiers in sight. Our orphanage Mother and her devoted staff members capitalize on the ceasefire, trying to find a way to sneak us out through the back of the building. They lead us to a rickety Volkswagen bus. It has no air conditioner, and the tires are barely hanging on, but we quickly pile in until no lap or inch of floor remains unoccupied. Our belongings flap in the wind, strapped to the roof of the vehicle as we rush to get out of Gbarnga before another attack. Steadily, we make our way to a new orphanage in Monrovia.

After all of this, who am I?

I'm starving.

Barely alive.

But the bus is rolling, so I must keep going forward.

What's in a Name?

"What's in a name?" begs the famous line out of Shakespeare's play *Romeo and Juliet*. "That which we call a rose by any other name would smell as sweet."[1] Juliet is clearly complaining because she can't associate with Romeo, the love of her life, due to the family name he carries. To her relatives, the name represents danger, as these two families have been longstanding enemies. But to Juliet, Romeo's last name is meaningless. He would be the same Romeo, even if he was called anything else, and she would still be in love with him.

You'd probably argue the same if you had always had a given name. You'd think you could still be the same person even if your parents had decided to call you something different, right? You'd share the same interests, have the same favorite color, love the same foods, make the same friends and relationships. You'd be everything you are today, just called something else. Because, a name is just a name.

Hopefully, I have you second-guessing this by now.

Truth is, names carry power. We even see this biblically. Adam, in the very first book of the Bible, Genesis, has a name handpicked by God that means "earth." He was literally made up of dirt and had life breathed into him by God. Mary is specifically instructed to give her son the name Jesus, "the name that is above every other name" (Phil. 2:9) and "'they will call him Immanuel' (which means 'God with us'" (Matt. 1:23).

There are times in the Bible when God changes people's names. This usually happens when He gives them a new calling. Abram (which translates to "exalted father") becomes Abraham (meaning "father of a multitude") as a confirmation of God's promise that Abraham will be just that, a father to many nations. Then there's Jacob, a twin born grasping his brother's heel, whose name closely translates to "heel grabber." After wrestling with God, Jacob's name is changed to Israel, which means "wrestles with God."

> **Truth is, names carry power.**

There are countless stories defending the power of names throughout the Bible. In each circumstance, people's names represent their identity. If their names are changed, it represents that they are not the same anymore. God has something new in store for them.

The same thing happened to me. At birth, I was named Cammué Mendawe Gweh. Cammué translates to "little giant." Some said that I was small and mighty, just like my namesake, my paternal grandfather. Mendawe means "the thing they want." And Gweh is the word for a "shekere cup* that holds water without any leakage."

In short, my full name meant "a small but strong, wanted, good vessel." Of course, that name would eventually be taken from me.

I'm not going to pretend to be an Abraham or a Jacob, but I do believe God renamed me because He wanted to do something new in me too.

What's Your Name?

Peeking my head out from behind the group of new orphans in Monrovia, I watch closely as one of the women questions us one by one. She writes down our full names, birthdays, and tribal associations. Standing a little more than halfway back in the long line, my stomach knots because, at seven years of age, I don't even know my full name. "Cammué" is all anyone has ever called me.

It's my turn and I nervously step forward.

"What's your name?" she asks.

I freeze. In a voice much quieter and weaker than I desire, I whisper, "Cammué."

"Cammué who?" she replies.

"I … I don't know." *Who am I at this point anyway? Does Cammué even exist anymore?*

A few minutes pass, and the woman returns. "Everyone in the home is required to have a first and last name," she states matter-of-factly. Then, her voice edges into a soft tone as she says, "You know, you remind me of one of Pastor Kofi's sons. Pastor Kofi runs this orphanage. His son unfortunately lost his life in a swimming accident at just your age. But that will be your name. Jackson. Jackson Kofi."

Jackson? Jackson. Sure. It's a very "civilized name," and I think it fits me pretty well. Jackson has seen war. Jackson has survived. Plus, it's easier to pronounce, despite the very little English I speak. When I am given the go-ahead, I sprint across the yard with the biggest smile on my face. I am eager to meet my friends and introduce the new me.

Hi, I'm Jackson Kofi now.

Yes, God is doing a new thing. My life will be better here.

———

Days have passed, and my hopes are not dashed. Life really is better here. This orphanage, in Monrovia, seems to be less than fifty miles from where I grew up, but I feel like I'm in another country. Big buildings and large roads surround us here! As a village boy, I've never seen the city before. I'm a city boy now, and I like it!

I am also having my first glimpse at family in a while. Truthfully, I have never had any perception of a stable family because my parents were never married. Before I ever lost my parents in the war, I had already learned to consider other people a part of my family—even if we didn't share the same blood. I see older women as mothers or aunties, older men as father figures, and other kids as brothers or sisters.

In the orphanage, each "home" has one superior "Mother" whom everyone reports to. I'm particularly fond of one of the Mothers over at the girls' dorm. She's rather fond of me too and cares for me most. Below her are "Caregivers"—elderly women who are respected in their community. We also have a male "dean" of the home. These people are now my family.

Since the orphanage has a buddy system, I'm also in charge of several younger boys, who look up to me as their older brother. It's honestly a pretty cool relational system.

While I have a sense of belonging here, I do still dream of my real family. I long for the whole pretty picture of a mom and dad again, smiling as they lovingly hold me and my siblings. We all live together in a beautiful home somewhere, happily ever after. It's a fairy tale. One I can only dream in my imagination. A real family isn't and may never again be my reality. So I'm grateful to God for the one I have found here. I pause and give thanks for my new name, Jackson. It means "God is gracious and merciful." Yes, He is.

Who am I?
I'm Jackson now.
And I keep going forward.

Provision in Poverty

War is coming again. I've been running for my life for two years now, and at nine years old, I've become numb to war.

Our Mother thinks it's a good idea to migrate the orphans to an area outside the city. She is hoping to keep us safe because the rebels seem to be out for anyone and everyone at this point. The city has become a hot spot for violence, and it's only a matter of time before Monrovia becomes a target.

By this point, I'm numb to moving. A low-grade sense of fear always surrounds me, so I don't flinch when I'm transferred to yet another orphanage, this one in Barnersville, a small town located several miles away from the city. Here, we'll seek refuge. Again.

On our way to settle in a safer area, I stare through the bus window as bombs explode beyond our remote, unpaved road. Guns fire in the distance as the two fighting groups draw near. I can't see the soldiers yet, but I imagine they are just on the other side of the field. The sounds of war become louder, and I'm scared. Always scared.

While we aren't in the direct line of fire, deadly struggles still threaten us. Our good streak has apparently ended because, by the time we left Monrovia, we had run out of food and provisions.

Our basic needs are no longer covered. If the rebels don't get us, starvation might.

Months have gone by in Barnersville, but it seems as if time is now in slow motion. We have no food in storage, and no donations are coming in at this point. We are so far gone that we are forgotten. The staff, my fellow orphans, and I are left to our own devices as we struggle to make ends meet. I've become dehydrated from the hot sun, and my energy level has dropped so low that I'm constantly shaking. The consistent growl in my stomach has become white noise. I don't even notice it anymore.

Sitting down, I press my thumbs between my eyebrows and push them out across my forehead, as if it will ease my never-ending headache. My legs won't move. My short life begins to flash before my eyes as I consider giving in to the void and dying. "God, help us!" I cry.

As if He actually hears me this time, God shows me a way. He points me to a nearby forest and an unnoticed, forgotten farm where plantains are growing. I hike through the forest to find a small supply of bananas, guavas, plums, mangoes, limes, and lemons—like manna from heaven. A bounty of rotting fruit has fallen from forgotten trees into thick leaf piles. The locals who live in this area do not allow anyone to intrude on their farms but, in my current state of mind, I do not care. This plot seems abandoned, plus rules and farm etiquette went out the window a long time ago.

Only able bodies may leave the orphanage to hunt or gather extra food. It's survival of the fittest, and I want us all to live, so I rush to tell my other "able-bodied" friends. Together, we sneak into the bush and gather anything and everything that is edible—roots, leaves, lemons, rotten fruit, dead mice, and lizards. We set traps with hopes of catching possums, deer, and squirrels. We will take anything we can get our hands on.

A bell rings from afar. It's 5:30, and it's time for dinner. Restored to hope and now believing our fortune can possibly change, I sprint back to the orphanage optimistic that somehow God also allowed donations to come through and we will have some rice, cornmeal, or bags of wheat for supper. Maybe those who couldn't join us in the farm raids will have some sustenance tonight. Our bellies could feel full for the first time in years!

My hope is in vain. Warm water is the only thing on the menu. Again. It washes down the dead mouse I had eaten in the woods, desperate for a source of protein. At least I had something to eat.

Our Mother gathers everyone around in the dining hall. We hold hands as she prays over the warm water. She encourages us to keep trusting God and ask Him to provide His children the nutrients we need to survive.

Oh, God.

Amen.

Weeks have gone by. There's still no food. Other orphans have joined in on our farm raids, so there's nothing to eat now except the clay from the swamp and roots from my secret cassava* patch. I didn't think I could get any weaker, but I am. My steps are slower. My strength has almost completely faded. From recent bowel movements, I've discovered I have parasitic worms. I cry for my mom, forgetting that she's not here. Sometimes I think I can conjure her up if she can hear the pain and suffering in my voice. I whimper. I see her in hallucinations, but she never comes to rescue me. I feel like I'm decomposing while alive. All I can do now is say a prayer to God, commit to Him my life and soul, and wait for my turn to die. I'm just waiting.

Eventually, we hear news of a ceasefire. Now that the war has died down for a bit, our Mother gathers us all, and we make our way back toward the city in hopes that, with more access to resources, life will be better for us there. This time we find shelter in an old school building at the King James Orphanage.

> Who am I?
> I'm dying.
> But the will to live keeps me moving forward.

The King James Orphanage is located back in the Monrovia and ELWA Junction area. It's made up of two abandoned buildings next to a stream of running water and a swamp. One building is used for schooling, devotions, and meetings. It's less run-down, so the girls sleep there. The boys and I live in a smaller building next door. It's covered in green algae. We sleep on the concrete floor with our shirts under our chests to protect our ribs from the rough ground.

They tell us we are prone to disease here because of the tainted water. We can get bacterial infections from bloodsucking mosquitoes and flies too. But I'm accustomed to this environment. At least here we can hunt for food in the swamp. And I'll take a bug over a bullet any day.

Creek fishing doesn't feed us much, and the starvation rate is through the roof. The government stopped supplying food or any aid to us. I'm dumb and desperate, so I often climb up from our room's ceiling into the storage room to steal rice.

We have no pots or a stove to cook the rice, so my friends and I search the dumpster for large tomato cans. We gather debris, twigs, and coal. Then we start a small fire inside some broken cement blocks we've found at an abandoned house up the street. Once the fire is going, we put the can of rice atop the blocks and let it boil. Sometimes the rice comes out burned, and other times it's halfway cooked. Regardless, we always eat it. We have no choice. It's the only food we've got.

If you're counting, you know I've been moved to four different orphanages now. And I'm about to be transferred once more. Don't worry. This will be my last time.

So far, this journey has been a bit dark, right? Gah, I know. But don't worry. You've already made it through the roughest scenes in my story, so thanks for hanging in there with me. The Light will come, I promise. My whole life and the tone of this book is about to change.

Our Mother just received word that another of Pastor Kofi's orphanages, the Monrovia Home for Orphans and Indigenous Children, has space for some of us there in a city called Sinkor, just a few blocks away from the Liberian president's executive mansion. In order to lower the death rate here and offer surviving children more food, a group of us who were first at Miss Evelyn's orphanage are being transferred to this new location. Once again, I load onto a bus with my peers, and off we go into another unknown future.

When we pull up to the new orphanage, I can't believe my eyes. In comparison to where I've been over the past couple of years, Monrovia Home is a resort. It's fenced in, with a security guard, and has a large yard to play in, just steps away from the ocean. We are appointed a "Mission Mother" who will watch over us. Then, we are each assigned to our dormitories, one for boys and one for girls. There's a separate building for dinner, devotions, and large gatherings. There is even a well on-site to provide safe drinking water. It was built by missionaries who were active supporters of Pastor Kofi's vision and the orphanage.

I love Monrovia Home. We finally have plenty of food here, and I feel safe. Tangibly, with every meal and laugh and song, I can feel life coming back into my bones. Now resurrected, I play and feel like a kid again most days.

I have found brothers and sisters here too. Daniel is my "older brother" now because he has taken me in as his own. Rufus is my "brother" because he's become my very best friend. Felicia and Tina are my "sisters," and I spend most of my days at Monrovia playing with them.

The girls pretend to make dinner for Rufus and me, serving us sand that looks like rice as they mash up flower petals for grains or soup. Our real meals are prepared for us in a can-shaped, oversize pot in a similar fashion. Typically, rice, water, and mashed flower petals are mixed together to form a brown, murky, soup-like mixture. The pot is then placed on top of three sturdy triangular pieces of rock and cooked over tiny pieces of debris set aflame in place of firewood.

Sometimes the rice cooks well. Other times, when I get a serving from the bottom of the pot, it's crunchy or burned, and I think our pretend dinner may have actually tasted better. But I'm not complaining because here, we're fed!

The only downside is that, just like everything else on our side of the world, the orphanage has been touched by the war. Bullet holes can be seen throughout the property, and a gap in the fence marks the spot where a bomb exploded. The hole leads straight out to the beach. While the ocean is beautiful, we often use it as a bathroom because there's not much room in the orphanage for us all. I always watch my step. A few feet away from the shore are thick sea bushes where human remains still lie. The breeze wafts in the smell of rotting bodies. It's become a familiar aroma, one that marks most of my memories at this point. Sometimes I don't even notice it anymore.

Despite being constantly surrounded by reminders of death and war, I begin to think that I may survive after all. I'm coming back to life.

Who am I?
God be praised, I'm alive!
I really can keep moving forward.

Meet Pastor Kofi

You've heard the name Pastor Kofi a couple times now, and to understand my story, you have to meet him. So let me introduce you.

Pastor Kofi was there from the beginning of it all. He was there at the start of the war. He was on the front lines of creating orphanages and safe havens for children like me. Children who were dying. Children with no parents. Children who were living on the streets. And he was there to help me pen the first chapters of my survival story.

His ministry and work saved me and countless other children, so I can't really go any further without telling you a little bit more about the father we all found when we didn't have one.

While writing this book, I had the honor of interviewing Pastor Kofi at his stateside office in Lancaster, South Carolina. It's always been so interesting to me that this man started a ministry all the way across the ocean in Liberia and it somehow found a second home in a small southern American town not even an hour from where I currently live. But we'll talk more about that in a second.

For now, picture a cloudy, chilly spring day. I turn down the old gravel road that leads to the stateside home base of African Christians Fellowship International (ACFI). Pastor Kofi's ministry and church consist of a small, plain, humble brick building that gives nothing away as far as the grand miracles that have spilled over from the inside.

I arrive with my friend Kaley, who is helping me navigate this book. She and I are greeted at the door by the friends I still consider family. Pastor Kofi's adult son embraces me first and hands me his six-month-old baby boy. I hold the infant close, as if he's one of my own. We all laugh and catch up for a moment in the small entryway until Pastor Kofi signals us back to his office.

Everything is wooden and unassuming, a simple chair and desk for such a deep and complex character. Pastor Kofi's kind face is backdropped by the built-in shelves bulging with unorganized books. He's just as I remember him, with rich ebony skin, glasses that recline on his face as if they've been there his whole life, and a genuine smile that stretches from ear to ear. He seats us and starts sharing his story in a soft, full voice that flows as smooth and thick as honey.

Kaley takes notes and records our conversation as we both hang on to Pastor Kofi's every word. Here's a summary of all he shared with us.

Tshainfuer Edward Kofi was born into a big native-Liberian family of two parents and ten children, all suffering in slavery and forced labor from Americo-Liberians. Tensions were incredibly high between indigenous and non-native peoples; village life was, as it always seems to be, insanely hard. There was little transportation and no school. His parents believed the only way out was through education. If they could get one child educated, this kid could not only be the breadwinner but a representative for their family. Kofi was honored to be chosen by his parents and sent to a foster home where he was promised he would attend school and be well taken care of.

Surprisingly, things turned bad quickly.

Kofi wasn't sent to school and was, instead, abused from the ages of six to twelve years old. Eventually he'd had enough. He needed to break free from the living situation that had become a prison, so he had to make a hard decision that no child should ever have to make. Kofi had to choose between staying in the home to be assaulted or running away and living on the streets of Monrovia.

He ran.

Quickly, Kofi adapted to life as a street child, doing whatever it took to stay alive. Finally, his parents got word of just how far south their plan had gone, and his dad went to rescue him. Little did he know, God was also coming to his aid. God had something special up His sleeve for when this prodigal son would return home.

While Kofi was surviving on the streets, an engineer in America (Longview, Texas, to be exact) heard a plea for help from the Liberian president at a US conference and decided to offer aid by creating a ministry hub in Liberia. He brought massive excavating machines and a few missionary families to come and live in close proximity to Kofi's village. The mission group launched a school, hosted job trainings, and began spreading the message of Jesus. Kofi's parents believed that if he could be sent there, his life could be redeemed.

Turns out, they weren't wrong.

At twelve years old, Kofi ventured to the ministry hub and discovered God did have a great plan for his life. He finally started school and began to learn about the Word of God. He quickly accepted Jesus as his Lord and Savior through his missionary Sunday school teacher. He also took advantage of the opportunities for job training. He learned to be a mechanic and began to practice medicine. *What can't this man do?*

By the time he finished junior high, the mission hub was closing (for reasons he still doesn't fully know). So Kofi returned to the city of Monrovia to begin high school. He was returning to the big city as a completely different person than he was when he'd left. Now he was older, wiser, and full of the love of Jesus.

Defying all the odds, this village boy had survived the worst, graduated from high school, and was now studying medicine with big dreams of becoming a doctor. However, the more steps he took into the medical field, the more he could feel God pulling him in a different direction.

He couldn't stop thinking about the Americans who had left behind their lives full of comfort to come serve struggling Liberians. He could tell it wasn't pity that had brought them to this ministry base in a faraway land. It was the love of God that had led them to serve those in need, and he wanted to follow in their footsteps.

There was a call on his life that he couldn't deny anymore. He needed to help his people. Kofi decided then and there that he too wanted to be a missionary.

He believed God's path for him led back home. So he returned to his rural village as a young man and served in the government as a municipal commissioner for the next seven years.

And here's where our stories are about to collide.

The 1980s brought on a new era for Kofi and, in 1986, he birthed the organization that would become my home, ACFI. Kofi began training young adults and had God-sized goals of reaching the entire nation of Liberia with the gospel. Following shortly on the heels of his mission launch, the infamous military coup took place, and Liberia's government was overthrown.

I know what you're thinking. This is where I tell you something about how this dark spot in Liberian history began to overshadow ACFI and that they had to persevere through utter hardship. However, the complete opposite happened.

Here's the wildest thing about the kingdom of God—most things are backward from our earthly assumptions or understandings. Almost every time in history, when there is great persecution, the church and its ministries thrive. ACFI was no exception. The ministry grew at a rapid pace, creating more than three hundred churches in eight cities throughout the subregion of West Africa. Despite the country being tossed into the fires of a great civil war, Kofi remained faithful. In typical fashion when a person or place is favored by God, ACFI defied every odd and thrived.

While God was blessing ACFI, evil was wreaking havoc on Liberia. The war was escalating, and Kofi's vision for ACFI began to pivot as he took note of the mental, physical, and spiritual state of the children he was caring for. He could see a glint of his former sense of loss, devastation, and hopelessness reflected in the darkening eyes of every kid who had been forced out on the streets to survive. He understood their pain and knew he had to do everything he could to save them.

His heart was breaking as truckloads of kids began showing up at the ACFI mission compound headquarters. The Liberian president, Samuel Doe, and his wife were even risking their own lives by going to villages, finding lost children, and bringing them to the ACFI doorstep. The mission had no other choice but to open their doors to the masses of children that God was bringing to them and pray that if God was multiplying, He'd also be providing. So they began to start orphanages around the city of Monrovia.

Unfortunately, one of the main terror tactics of the rebel armies was to locate orphanages, break in, and abuse or rape the children. If they could ingrain fear in children, they could keep power for generations to come. After a few of the ACFI homes became victims of these raids, Kofi made a plan to partner with American supporters to build one compound that could hold all the children. The ACFI team could then watch over all the orphans at the same place with hopes of keeping them safe.

Once again, God opened doors. Literally. As a result of donors' sincere generosity and prayer, orphanages were built, including Daniel Hoover Children's Village (or Monrovia Home, as it was formerly called and as you've seen it referenced in this book so far), and 518 children were transported to these safe homes from across the greater Monrovia area. *Remember, I was one of them!*

All of us who lived there lacked nothing because American churches and donors not only supported ACFI with everything the children needed, they also came to visit, serve, and care for those in the home. Some of these visiting families formed a tight bond with specific kids and wanted to offer them a better life. So Kofi also launched an adoption program out of ACFI. *Genius.*

This is where I come in. Pastor Kofi and I crossed paths through his belief that children had gifts that could be developed to praise the Lord. He thought I could sing …

What Happens When You Sing through Suffering

The famous trumpeter and vocalist Louis Armstrong once stated, "Music is life itself."² And the psalmist declared, "My lips will shout for joy when I sing praise to you—I whom you have delivered" (Ps. 71:23).

Whether you're a master musician or someone who just likes to crank up your favorite song in the car, I think we can all agree God placed within music the power to change things—our situations, perspective, emotions, and heart. All it takes is the right chord progression or song lyric, and everything can shift.

At least, it did for me. Along with food and safety, music revived my soul and ultimately changed the entire trajectory of my life.

If you're feeling hopeless today, have lost your sense of identity, or are struggling to survive this season, I get it. I've been there and know these feelings more than I want to admit. However, when I had nothing else, God gave me music. He gives you music too. So whistle a tune, turn up your favorite song, or belt a melody. You never know what could shift. I sure didn't.

"Never Lord, are You too far away. You did not bring me up this far to let me down." My voice would ring out the lyrics, preaching to myself through one of my favorite songs that the choir guys and I had written. In those moments when I was singing, God reminded me of my identity in Him. He loved me. He was protecting me. And I began to sing my way out of the dark.

Here's how …

Sing a Song

There are strict rules that we all have to follow at Monrovia Home.
One of those guidelines is that we have to attend the ACFI church
where Pastor Kofi preaches every Sunday. It's about a twenty-minute
walk, but I don't mind it so much. The church is located only a few
steps away from the beach so, afterward, I stroll along the shoreline
quietly and peacefully back to the orphanage.

As if my thoughts are like the grains of sand sifting through my
toes, I use the time to sort through my prayers and think on notes
from the sermon. I can truly feel God's presence like I never have
before in my life. We used to have to walk so incredibly far to hear
the gospel preached in my other villages. But here, it's close. God is
so close. And I'm using every opportunity to draw nearer to Him.

Here at our new orphanage, we fast and attend revivals. Another
rule is that we must participate in devotional time in the morning
before breakfast and at night after dinner before bed. I'm almost a
teenager. So, like any good adolescent on the brink of adulthood,
part of me likes the thrill of breaking the rules or pushing boundaries
just a bit. Okay more than a bit. A lot. But this is one rule I actually
don't want to test.

> When I had nothing else,
> God gave me music. >>>>>

I stay in the lines here because I genuinely want to be at devotions every day. It's this incredible time when I get to hang out
with my friends. We worship together and lean on each other as we
belly-laugh at jokes to pass the time away. In these moments, the

hardships we are all facing disappear. We're simply together; we're just kids being kids, and that's all that matters.

The leaders and my peers here are unlike any other people I've ever been around in my life. They're positive, uplifting, and full of life and energy. There's no time here to sit and complain about our struggles or what we lack. We are thankful. We are taught to be a light in the darkest places, and everyone around me is truly living that out. Every night we compete to see who can quote the most Scriptures from the Bible. Guess what? I crush it! Our team has been winning the past couple of matches (we lost once to the pastor's son, but that doesn't count, right? A pastor's kid is supposed to win).

I'm seeing God at work, and I've never experienced anything like this. There is more for me. I'm coming back to life!

Let's Start a Choir!

It's devotion time and we have two options. We can either share our testimony or sing a song. Talking about my story isn't my favorite thing, for obvious reasons, so I always choose to sing. I've been making mental notes of others who are making the same choice. Just then, my friend Steve stands to sing.

Hey, I recognize this song! Taking the tenor line, I jump in. Not to toot my own horn or anything, but I can tell everyone in the room is enjoying it.

"Jackson, I didn't know you had beautiful vocals like I do, brother," Steve gloats afterward. "We should do this every night."

"Yeah, we should!" I'm in full agreement.

Worship is amazing, and we begin to draw interest from other kids from the Home. Their enthusiasm leads us to a bright idea—what if we pull together all the boys around our age who like to sing? We can create an all-boys acapella choir!

Some new (or maybe long-forgotten) feeling, sparks in me at the thought of singing together with my friends. Something like JOY!

We get started by bringing our group together to practice in our rooms at night and to set some strict standards. We establish the following choir rules:

1. You must have some sort of musical talent or desire to learn. On top of that, you cannot be stiff, timid, or too shy to express your gratitude to God through worship.
2. If you miss practice twice, then you must return to your seat with the congregation.
3. Learn and fully memorize all the songs and vocal parts, and always attend devotions.

I know. These rules might seem a little over the top to some of the guys, but, hey, we're passionate about protecting our newfound joy.

It's been a few months, and we now have a grand total of twelve boys in the choir. I'm no expert, but I'd say we're pretty good. The visiting mission group thinks so too. Even Pastor Kofi agrees that we're doing a good job. So good, in fact, that he sat down with us the other night to tell us some incredible news. He shared his vision with the mission group that was just here visiting. They want to send us to America!

He's also hired two choir directors at the church to help get us prepared. Under their direction, we practice three times a day, learning more than three to five new songs a day. Collectively we write about twenty songs, not including the countless ones we already know.

I can't believe it. The Liberian Acapella Boys Choir is headed to the States on tour!

Families are hugging and wishing each other safe travels in the airport. I haven't seen open affection shared between a parent and child in so long that it makes my heart ache. Suddenly, I'm keenly aware of the fact that there is no one here to tell me goodbye. No mother. No father. No siblings or cousins. *Will I ever see them again? Will I ever return to Liberia?*

I didn't know so many opposite emotions could exist inside me at once. My heart feels like it could leap out of my chest with excitement while, at the same time, fear and deep sadness sit like a rock in my gut. Tears are trying to well up in my eyes while the corners of my mouth can't keep from smiling.

Turning toward the plane, I walk with the only family I do have, my choir brothers, into an unknown future. It's only up from here.

> Who am I?
> I'm Jackson, and I'm going to America!
> So, I keep moving forward.

Section 3

WELCOME TO AMERICA

This is my story, this is my song
Praising my Savior all the day long ...

Fanny Crosby, "Blessed Assurance"

As our plane descends into Washington, DC, ice forms intricate patterns across my window. Still buckled into my seat, I trace God's frozen masterpieces along the glass, and my fingers tingle at the excitement of it all. This is not only my first flight; it's also my first cold-weather experience. My first time out of Liberia. So many firsts!

The plane lands, and I'm finally in the country that I've dreamed of for so many years. What will America be like? I gaze out at this new land, and she, in all her stunning beauty and glory, smiles back at me.

The sun is starting to go down as we grab our overhead bags and shuffle with our fellow travelers off the plane. We immediately head toward baggage claim to look for Pastor Kofi's oldest son, who has been assigned to guide our choir group. He is like a celebrity to us because he came here to America in a choir before ours. They recorded a cassette tape that was sent back to us in Liberia. We listened to that tape over and over. I'm thrilled to meet and be shown around this great country by a big brother and ACFI choir celebrity we all love and respect.

As we head toward the carousels, where hundreds of suitcases swirl around the conveyor belt, each belonging to other world travelers, we bump right into our dark-complected, acapella-music-loving mentor. *There is Pastor Kofi's son!* He gathers us together and instructs us to grab our luggage and head toward the parking garage. With few belongings to call our own, we have all traveled light. So it takes us only a moment to grab our single, barely full bags and head out.

The doors slide open, and we make our long-anticipated, grand entrance onto American soil. Bold and confident, I begin to strut through this wide-open door of opportunity when … *What was that?* The most frigid blast of wind I've ever felt just hit me, taking my breath away. *This is the cold everyone back home told me about.* All the boys in the choir shiver with me. In one look, we communicate an action plan. Then we take off running on frozen legs back into the warmth of the terminal. There, we open our small suitcases and, as fast as we humanly can, throw on all the clothes we have with us. While this outfit will make for less than a grand entrance, I'm much warmer in the layers.

Let's try this again. We exit the doors more humbly this time, knowing we stick out like a sore thumb. Almost immediately a long fifteen-passenger burgundy van pulls up to greet our mismatched Liberian crew. Pastor Kofi's son and the American ACFI team are ready to take us to our home away from home.

Excitedly, we pile into the van while we joke about everyone's reaction to the cold air. Our laughter subsides into a few slow, sparse chuckles and is slowly replaced with an awkward discomfort. My mind races. *What do we do now that we're in America? How are we supposed to act? What if the people hate us here?* As if our driver can read our minds, he starts to blast African music and Afrobeats. I relax at the sound of something familiar, and so do my friends. We sing along together as the driver pulls out of the terminal.

America, here we come!

Kentucky Fried Chicken

The bus takes a sharp turn into a parking lot where a small red-and-white building stands alone. Some cars are parked in the front parking lot. Others wait in a slow-moving line that wraps around the side of the building. *What are the cars doing there? Are they seriously talking into that box?* Everyone in the bus exchanges curious glances. "What is this place?" we all ask at almost the exact same time. We start cracking up again, the way young kids do when they're so excited they turn silly.

"What is this place?" our driver sarcastically echoes. "It's called KFC!"

We all look dumbfounded. I've never heard of anything remotely close to "KFC" in my life, and clearly my friends haven't either.

"What's KFC?" I ask.

"Y'all get out of the car, and you'll find out," he says with a twinkle in his eye.

We can tell it must be something special, so we dart out of the van and head toward the front door as fast as we can. Inside, I realize that KFC is something amazing, something I've only heard of but never seen—a restaurant. It's beautiful, clean, and … *upscale? Is that the word I'm looking for?* Whatever it is, my first impression is that KFC is fancy!

Beyond the big windows in the dining area, roads and bridges cross over one another. Vehicles of all colors and sizes speed by in multiple lanes. *We've made it! We've made it to heaven!*

I'm pulled out of a daze when, out of the corner of my eye, our driver and a KFC employee come walking toward us with red-and-white-striped buckets of fried chicken. I've never tasted fried chicken before, but it smells so delicious my mouth is already watering. We each grab a bucket and, at the first bite, our wide eyes and big smiles confirm—yes, this is the best food we've ever had.

I'm not sure when we'll get food again. Maybe America is like Liberia? I should probably save some for later. I take out a napkin and wrap some of my chicken before stuffing the leftovers in my pocket for later. Then I head back out toward the van, blissfully full.

I can't sleep. We're all stuffed from our American-sized feast of KFC chicken. Plus, I'm exhausted from our overnight flight. My choir brothers doze, but I remain wide-eyed during the six-hour drive toward the ACFI base in Lancaster, South Carolina. Like a kid gazing through a candy-shop window, I can't help but stare at all the cars and highway signs and think that America looks sweet.

Finally, after bumping down a rural dirt road for a while, we arrive at a farmhouse owned by our church sponsor, First Church. We jump out of the van and race toward the two-story cabin. It looks like a mansion to us, and it even has a pool in the backyard. *A pool! I've never seen that before.* With two floors and several bedrooms, there's plenty of space for all of us. Plus, it's only a few minutes' walking distance to the church. I'm going to settle in nicely here.

I could fill this whole book with hundreds of pages of memories of my experiences in America. There were so many "firsts" for me here. My first warm shower. My first time feeling the air-conditioning. My first tastes of lots and lots of new foods. I don't want to bore you with all the details of me being culture shocked in all the best ways. So I'll cut to the chase with just two main "first stories" that you need to know before we hop over to the plot twist God wrote in my life.

Goodwill

As you remember, we arrived in America with very little luggage and had layered most of our clothing onto our backs when we experienced our first fall breeze at the airport in Washington, DC. But with a year-long choir tour coming up, we all need clothes.

There is no way Pastor Kofi can afford to take all twelve of us shopping while trying to feed all the mouths in the orphanage and raise awareness for his ministry. But God is a provider. So we aren't surprised when He comes through for us, like He always does.

We are invited to sing a small performance (like a practice for the big concerts we have coming up) for a local church in Lancaster.

After the service, the preacher collects a "love offering" from their generous congregation. With that money, a very sweet, elderly lady loads us all up in our van and takes us to a very fine clothing establishment that I now know as Goodwill.

"You can each select a few outfits," she instructs our group.

She doesn't have to tell me twice. Immediately, I start grabbing random shirts and pants. At this moment, I feel so rich. This is the most access I've ever had to anything. I am King Midas. Everything I touch feels like gold, and I can't thank God enough for all the treasure He is giving to us.

I recall that memory now and wish I could experience again what such extreme gratitude feels like. With access to so much "stuff" here in America, it's easy to lose our sense of appreciation for it all. Even for you as a reader, the fact that you could buy this book puts you in a class of wealth most of the world will never experience.

That's why I fight every day to remain extremely grateful. I never want to forget that we are insanely blessed. There are so many golden gifts from God right in front of us on prosperity's path, but we step right over them because we're not looking at the countless blessings He provides for us every day.

I'm here to say, we should start looking. Noticing. And appreciating the bounty He offers.

Shoe Show

Following our Goodwill treasure hunt, the same sweet, elderly lady takes us to a second shopping location. The van door opens, and she gives us another jaw-dropping announcement. "Everyone can have a pair of shoes. Don't worry about paying. It's on me."

My eyes open wide as we enter a store called Shoe Show. Never have I seen so many shoes in one place. There was nothing, and I mean nothing, like this in Liberia. Did this lady really say I could have my choice of any of them? Boy, I am pumped about getting a pair of Shaq's Dunkman Style 34 basketball shoes. Maybe then I can learn to play American basketball with my neighbors.

Out of the corner of my eye, I spot a pair of clean, white kicks. As fast as I can, I run over and slip my feet out of my tattered shoes and straight inside the fresh, new pair. I stare at my feet for a long moment. "New shoes on my feet" is something I have never seen or felt before. After taking in the vision, I exhale as a wide grin spreads across my face. These shoes are perfect. No one could possibly have found a cooler pair than me.

I swagger back onto the bus and join the rest of the crew in smack-talking about who has the most "dope" shoes until one of the guys starts busting out laughing at me.

"What? What's so funny?" I ask.

"Jackson," he says, "your shoes have a 'W' on the tag, bro."

I can't yank the shoe back fast enough. "No way!"

Sure enough, I lift the tag to see a 'W' glaring back at me. The whole bus erupts in laughter. But I don't really care. They can laugh all they want. I have new shoes!

I will wear these fresh, white women's shoes proudly every single day.

First Concert, First Church

It's Saturday. Some of the ACFI men are here at the farmhouse along with Pastor Kofi. We have our first real concert tonight at First Church, the church that has been hosting our stay in America. Pastor Kofi gives us a lecture that starts with the history of the church, rises at their role in our adventure, and ends in a motivational speech on the importance of this concert and our mission here in the States. *Man, that guy can give a talk.*

"You are missionaries," he says. "You are sent by your brothers and sisters in the orphanage to raise sponsorship and awareness for our country and friends back in Liberia." He doesn't have to expound too much; our hearts are already exploding with passion and excitement. God is going to do something big, and we can all feel it.

> Our hearts are already exploding with passion and excitement.

After the men leave, we practice our choir performance and go over a game plan for Sunday. Nervous energy fills the air. None of us has ever performed for a crowd full of White, American people before. *How receptive will they be to us?*

Despite our doubts, we are ready. We are confident because we have spent months going over every pitch, tune, and move. We meticulously iron our custom-made choir uniforms—emerald-green and white embroidered dashiki* with black pants and solid black shoes. We check out our new haircuts in the bathroom mirror we all share. Then, we make a list of who will shower first, based on who takes the longest showers and who barely bathes. *Don't worry, I'm somewhere in the middle.*

The rule is that we must be settled in bed by ten o'clock, but our excitement leaves most of us awake until midnight. I lean back lazily on my bed and listen to the guys talk back and forth while others doze. One of the older members of our group yells, "Hush it. Time to call it a night." With this, the room finally falls quiet and, humming a line from a concert piece in my mind, I drift off to sleep.

Greedy Gut

It's Sunday morning. We're focused and sharp, waiting with anticipation in the back room at First Church. It's only been about ten minutes by the time Pastor Kofi opens the door, but it feels both like an eternity and like no time has passed at all. He gathers us together in a huddle to pray. His "amen" is shortly followed by a voice booming from a microphone in the sanctuary.

"Everyone, please stand and help us welcome, all the way from Liberia, West Africa, the Liberian Acapella Boys Choir!" The pastor might as well have been an announcer at a stadium concert. My heart races. It's go time!

The entire congregation of about one hundred fifty people is standing, clapping, and smiling. Before I know it, we are coming through the back door and our lead singer is sparking up our walk-in song. As the lead singer, Steve looks left and right to assign each vocal group our pitch. He counts down and then raises his voice in the tune of the first song. We start singing along, our confidence building as we make our way to the stage.

The concert continues, and we are nailing it. Our rhythm is on point, vocals sound heavenly, and some of the boys break out their best dance moves. They even grab a member from the congregation to dance and sing with us. The crowd loves it. So much so that at the end of our six songs, the church is shouting, "One more! One more!" The bit of English I learned in school is enough for me to understand exactly what they are saying. *They want an encore? I can't believe it.* We've killed it.

I'm on cloud nine as we head to meet the congregation after our performance. It's clear on the faces of everyone in the choir that we are beaming from a job well done. Congregants come by and hug our necks, hold our hands, and let us play with their kids. I feel like a celebrity when I'm asked to take a picture with my new friends. I have never felt so loved and welcome in my life.

I thought I would be tired at the end of the morning, but I'm not. I'm fueled by such ecstatic energy as we walk back to the house to change into more comfortable clothes. Just before we get settled, Pastor Kofi surprises us with an invitation to join him and his family for lunch at the Chinese buffet just a few miles from the church. Who would say no to that? Pastor Kofi is a superhero to me. I will always agree to spending some time with him. The rest of the guys say yes too.

We sing in the van. I can tell by the way everyone is carrying on, we're going to be celebrating, jokingly criticizing each other's performances from the morning, and trying to learn the songs on the radio all the way to the Chinese restaurant.

The teasing and smack talking eases up as we pull into the parking lot on the corner of Main Street in downtown Lancaster. We all hop off the bus with high hopes that Chinese food is as delicious as it sounds. Pastor Kofi lets us know it's an "all you can eat" buffet. Apparently, that means you can get anything and everything you want. No limits!

My eyes grow wide at all the food options. Our entire choir of formerly starving children is suddenly paralyzed as we try to wrap our minds around the concept. I draw the conclusion that an "all you can eat" restaurant is presenting me with the challenge to see just how much I can eat. *Challenge accepted!*

We fill plate after plate with all kinds of exotic foods we never knew existed. I can't even pronounce the names of some of these options. *Who cares? It's amazing.* I'm still stuffing my face as the restaurant manager walks over to our long table. "Excuse me," he says. "You need to finish up and leave now."

He goes on to explain that we have eaten so much that his staff cannot keep up. There's not enough food left for the other patrons dining there.

Victory! We have conquered the all-you-can-eat buffet.

One of the guys doesn't hear the warning. He gets up to hop back in line for more fried plantains. The manager is fuming as he gathers some of his staff and returns to our table. Loud enough for the entire restaurant to hear, he orders us to "get out and never come back."

We shamelessly leave, laughing all the way out the front door, calling each other a title we so proudly just earned—"Greedy Gut."

All of us "Greedy Guts" are back at the cabin, sitting around the house, listening to music on a cassette player, Walkman, or portable CD player. Some people are also "burning CDs" like me, saving all my favorite slow jams and Celine Dion tracks. She's my favorite female artist, and I listen to her music when I need to soothe. Like lazy house cats, reclining in bed after a big meal, we're taking the afternoon to relax and relish the successful concert and buffet experience.

Before bed, we get a phone call that lets us know that we have a concert at a school at ten the following day. We need to be up and ready to go by eight thirty since the school is only a few miles away. Our choir calls together a meeting, and we start discussing what songs we want to sing tomorrow. We rehearse at least twice, and then we call it a night.

Good (Actually Really, Really Bad) Gravy

It's bright and early Monday morning, and our ACFI guide is outside waiting for us. I'm already dressed in my uniform—the African tribal shirt, black pants, and black shoes. We all seem to be carrying over a confident spirit from yesterday as we load up in the van. I think it's going to be another great day.

Upon our arrival, I quickly realize that this school is nothing like the schools we have in Liberia. The building is stunning, the grass is an immaculately manicured green, and the grounds are full of yellow buses and security guards. We park, and I'm awestruck as I start to make my way with the rest of the guys into the palace—I mean, building.

The principal is waving us over, so we all head in the direction he's pointing toward. He escorts us to the section of the school where the students await our arrival. I think he calls it an "auditorium." We enter and begin to take the stage. There are so many American faces just looking at us. With our cocoa-colored skin and African garb, maybe we look like aliens to them. We don't care.

Not one of us in this choir ever thought we would be in a place like this sharing our culture and music with people who have never set foot in Africa. Plus, they seem curious and overall excited to see and hear our testimonies through songs written in our native tongues. We run through the set flawlessly, just as we did the concert before, and exit the stage to a roar of applause.

We are immediately directed through the school to another new building I've never heard of called a "cafeteria." It's a big dining room with a lot of small tables and chairs where people cook meals in an industrial kitchen. They serve all kinds of very different American food, and this morning they are preparing breakfast for us—sausage, biscuits, and gravy. I don't know what any of that is, but it sounds great!

We don't normally have breakfast in Liberia. If we eat something in the morning, it's usually leftover rice, bread, butter, and tea mixed with canned milk and sugar. I stare down at my plate. This sausage gravy is nothing like what we know as "gravy" back at home. Bringing a bite up to my mouth, I try not to inhale. I hate the smell, and my stomach lurches. I want to throw up, but I don't. Apparently, I'm not the only one.

Several of the guys in the choir are pretending to eat or refusing to eat altogether. Out of the corner of my eye, I see Pastor Kofi get up, come over to them, and offer a speech that is motivational enough for them to start taking bites of the gray blobs wiggling on the plates in front of us.

I begin to conclude that maybe American food is great, but only for American people. It's processed, comes in cans and bottles, and almost everything has chemicals in it. *What's up with that?* Our Liberian bodies can't handle it. We are used to eating fruit fresh off the trees. At this thought, I can almost taste the leathery, sweet flesh of mango on the tip of my tongue. For a moment, I miss the taste of home.

We finally finish pretending to eat and load back up into the van. Waving goodbye to Indian Land High School, we pull out of the parking lot and head back to our house that has no mango trees.

Microwaved Ice Cream and Bucket Baths

These were the first two tour stops that really began to form for me what America and its culture looked like. I could tell you story after story about concerts and the people in each unique place, but I'll make this section short.

We had several tour stops in South Carolina and then made our way to Virginia, Maryland, Minnesota, and Tennessee. I'm sure we visited more places, but I can't remember them all. Sometimes after performing, it would be too late for us to drive back to Lancaster, so Pastor Kofi would ask families if they could take us in for the night. I really looked forward to staying in host homes. It definitely beat staying in the hotel with my crazy, loud, rice-eating choir brothers.

In host homes, I learned how African and American families differ. Typically, each American home was set at a pretty cold temperature, while we always kept the air off or at a high of seventy-five degrees. I struggled to sleep some nights because I was freezing, but I didn't know how to communicate that I needed another blanket or the air temperature turned up. This wasn't in my vocabulary yet, so I'd sleep in the African shirt I performed in and wear my boys choir sweatshirt on top as pajamas.

In the mornings, there wasn't leftover rice for breakfast but eggs, bacon, and grits. Grits was a new food for me, and I always thought it looked like rice after it had been cooked for an eternity. Surprisingly, I hated the way sausage smelled, and I thought milk was gross. To me, it had no taste. To this day, I still don't drink store-bought cow's milk. *Bleh.*

The hardest things for me to learn were names of household items, proper greetings, and table manners. I had never been introduced to any of these things. It was culture shock to say the least. Do you want to hear a few funny stories? I got you.

The first time I had ice cream, I thought it was too cold, so I put it in the microwave for three minutes.

When we were offered hot dogs at a church after one of our performances, we were appalled. *Absolutely not! We don't eat dogs!* The same thing happened with sandwiches. *No way! Who puts sand on bread? Gross.* We had to have several food items explained to us and were pleasantly surprised that a hot dog was just sausage in a bun. Not dog meat. Sandwiches were meat on bread. Sand was not a condiment. *Thank God!*

I would go days at a time without taking a shower because I never understood how to turn a shower knob. After trying to figure out how to work the odd-looking handle thingy for a while, I finally gave up, grabbed a bucket, located the nearest sink, and filled it with lukewarm water. Yes, instead of using the nice shower I had access to, I took a bucket bath.

Who am I?

I'm an African teen in an American world.

It's wild!

So, I keep moving forward.

Home Sweet Home?

In the days leading up to our tour stop at AME Zion Church, we're told that our one-year travel visas are about to expire. I'm getting ready for this next performance with that time clock ticking in the back of my mind. Soon I will have to go back to Liberia, to my old life. I pray this isn't the case. After being here for so long, I don't want to go back. And I'm not sure I know how to return to the world I left behind.

Our road manager and Pastor Kofi gather all twelve of us boys together and sit us down. Pastor Kofi then gets on his knees to deliver whatever message he's carrying. I can see in his eyes that this must be serious, so now I'm confused and curious. *Did God hear my prayer?* I lean in.

Pastor Kofi's voice is solemn. His heart is in his eyes as he shares that another war has erupted and we can't risk setting foot back in Liberia. If we were to land in Roberts International Airport, we would be killed the moment we exited the plane. It's impossible for us to go home. *Home. What is "home"?*

Reality starts to set in as I think of that word *home.* I haven't had a true home in years, and yet, when I close my eyes and think of where I belong, I picture Liberia. I see my mom and dad. I'm playing games with my brother. Yet none of them are here. None of them may even be alive anymore. "Home" doesn't exist for me. On the other hand, I don't have a home here either. *Where do I belong? Where do any of us belong? What even is a "home"?*

A wave of anxiety starts to roll over me. I'm tossed for a moment by intense worry and the disorienting notion of being displaced.

"Is there anything the American government can do to help extend our stay?" someone asks.

> I know God has a plan for my life. Desperately I long for Him to give me a family. >>>>>

"I'm not sure, son," Pastor Kofi replies honestly. "We will just have to trust God and continue to share our testimonies with our American brothers and sisters."

Any other day, this would be any other performance. We've been on tour for a while now, and I can sing our songs in my sleep. I could tell you exactly what every member of the choir is supposed to do and when we're each supposed to do it. We have become a unit, a well-oiled machine.

But this isn't any other day. Our lives have drastically changed. Soon we won't be able to go home—but also won't be able to remain here. We need God to come through for us, so every song we sing holds more emotion than it ever has before. We aren't just singing; we're crying out the lyrics. We're praying, begging for miracles.

"Never, Lord, are You too far away. You did not bring me up this far to let me fall," I beg God through song. I know God has a plan for my life. Desperately I long for Him to give me a family. *Don't let me go back to Liberia.*

Halfway through our performance, our tour manager takes the stage and delivers the gut-wrenching news to the congregation. He explains that our choir cannot return home in such dangerous conditions. We need help.

Where do we belong? I think again.

Little do I know, a lady in the audience is about to give us the answer.

Section 4
AN ORPHAN FINDS A HOME

God, I want to see You.
God, I want to hear You.
God, I want to know You.
God, I want to follow hard after You.
And even before I know what I will face today,
I say yes to You.

Lysa TerKeurst,
What Happens When Women Say Yes to God

Through the years of God making a way for me to come to America, there was a woman in North Carolina who thought her family was complete. She had a full life with raising three little girls, writing books to encourage other women, and running a nonprofit organization called Proverbs 31 Ministries.[1] Little did she know our two worlds were about to collide in an incredible way that only God could bring about.

People know her for a lot of things, and she's recognized by many titles. But for me, Lysa TerKeurst is the person who radically changed the course of my life by giving me a home. She was my kind and patient teacher, a woman determined to protect me and provide a home with enough safety to laugh and have fun again, and a brave soul who partnered with her family to take me in as one of their own. While Lysa has been so many things to me, my favorite title for her is simply "Mom."

All because one night, at a Liberian Acapella Boys Choir concert, she decided to give God a "yes."

We finish our song set, and the pastor takes the stage. "Let God work in your hearts," he says as he asks the audience to think about how they can all help our little Liberian brothers and sisters overseas. He prays over us, collects a love offering for the orphanage, and dismisses the church while we enter into our normal meet-and-greet session.

Almost instantly, I lock eyes with a dark-haired woman and her three daughters. I'm not sure if it's God who compels me or if my longing to have a mother figure back in my life is taking over, but I walk directly up to her and call out, "Mom!"

My best friend in the choir, Mark, does too. For a moment, we've found a family.

We start chasing the girls between the wooden pews. I'm laughing harder than I have in a while. Everything about our connection seems natural, as if we've all been best friends our entire lives. I can see the mom with the dark hair smiling at us. We play and play until it's time to go home.

Did you catch that? I instantly called the dark-haired woman my mom. Recently, I spoke to Lysa again about this moment, and she remembered it vividly. She said that instant felt like a divine appointment for her. She had been praying the prayer that I quoted at the top of this chapter every morning.

"God, I want to see you ... hear You ... know You ... follow hard after You. And even before I know what I will face today, I say yes to You."

She was in a daily habit of being very in tune with God and asking Him to reveal to her His bigger assignment. After she heard us call her "Mom," she couldn't unhear it. She knew God was calling her to support Mark and me. She just wasn't sure how.

On the way home, her daughters kept telling her to bring us home. We needed to be their brothers. I guess my mom and dad took their advice.

Sneaky Jesus

When I started writing this book, I couldn't wait to interview my mom. She held the whole backstory to my adoption process. As she started to share, we found out that Mark and I finding a home with the TerKeurst family was completely happenstance.

Get this. My sister was a Girl Scout at the time, and her troop had been studying different countries. She had been assigned to learn about Liberia. Lysa thought it would be fun to take her to our concert so she could meet Liberians firsthand. So they drove out to a little country church in the middle of nowhere with no expectations except to hear some music and maybe learn a few things about our home country.

A friend was sharing with me that one of her favorite women leaders in ministry, Annie F. Downs, calls this a "sneaky Jesus" moment. Just when we're not expecting it, in a totally ordinary moment, He sneaks in and does something extraordinary. A miracle is happening right under our nose without us having the slightest idea. It's sneaky in the best way, and Jesus sure was clever with the way He connected all of us that day.

Lysa jokingly confessed that she didn't even know where Liberia was on the map at the time. As she was talking about the assignment with her daughters, she told them to look in South America for it! My soon-to-be sisters quickly corrected her that it was, in fact, in Africa. Lysa played it off like she was just trying to keep them on their toes.

Clearly, no one—not her, not me, not Mark, not the pastor himself—could have seen this "sneaky Jesus" moment coming.

If you look at my mom's ministry, Proverbs 31, you can immediately tell she inspires people to live out their faith. She has always been that way. So after hearing our story, she shared with her then husband, Art, about everything. Initially he was hesitant.

Art has franchised a few Chick-fil-As in Charlotte, North Carolina. I clearly remember Lysa bringing Mark and me to the restaurant and introducing us to the man we would soon call Dad. After a few weeks, he warmed up to the idea, and they (thank God!) decided they were going to move forward with the adoption process.

But wait—it gets even better! Mark and I weren't the only ones adopted because of our encounter with the TerKeurst family. Lysa then brought Pastor Kofi and our entire choir to her church, where she told all her friends about our situation and prayed God would somehow make a way for the whole choir to be adopted.

> Even in my darkest hour, God had never left me or abandoned me. He had been working in the background all along. >>>>>

Guess what—they did! Almost all the members of the choir found homes in the Charlotte area of North Carolina!

Has this ever happened in the history of *ever*? An entire group of people came together to adopt preteen and teenage boys in the choir! Not only were we no longer orphans, we also all became (in a sense) actual brothers. We lived close to each other in Charlotte and got to grow up together. We also stayed connected to the only father figure we had through our childhood, Pastor Kofi, because his ACFI base in Lancaster wasn't too far away.

If the Bible were still being written today, this kind of thing might make it into the pages of Jesus' miracles. It would possibly serve as modern-day proof of John 14:18, when Jesus said, "I will not leave you as orphans; I will come to you."

I had a family in Christ. I now have a family with the TerKeursts. Even in my darkest hour, God had never left me or abandoned me. He had been working in the background all along.

Years earlier, I had cried out, "Mom!" when my orphanage was being raided. I thought no one had heard me. I had felt so alone and afraid. But it was almost as if God had preserved that outcry and released it years later, and Lysa answered back, "I'm here!"

Thank God for "sneaky Jesus."

A Scarcity Mindset in the Land of Abundance

It's been almost a decade since I've been able to call someone "Mom" and have her, a tangible flesh-and-bone human, respond. This all still feels like a dream. When I pictured the home of the TerKeursts, I imagined a sleek house in the city. Pleasantly, I am surprised as we pull down the long, obscure driveway to my new house. Like a countryside painting coming to life, the scene lights up before my eyes—a pond, a large field, and a beautiful, brick, two-story home set back in the woods.

As we step through the doorway for the first time, I ask *Mom* the first question that comes to mind. "Do I get my own bedroom?"

Guess what the answer is. "Yes!" Lysa replies.

My mouth immediately falls open and doesn't shut for the rest of the tour that the TerKeursts give us of their (I mean *our*) house.

We even have a weight room in our house! I've heard there are bullies in American schools. Now I'm going to be HUGE! No one will mess with me. Between this gym and the basketball hoop outside the house, I'll be in the best shape of my life.

There's also a pantry! I've never heard of a pantry before, but apparently it's the place where you store all your food. Who knew you could just keep food hanging around in your house and go grab it anytime you want? Amazing!

I'm quieter now than I ever have been, but I think it's because I'm still reminding myself that this is my real life. Taking everything in is like drinking through a fire hose. My mind is blown that I get to do crazy things like go to the grocery store with my *mom* and *brother*! I've never really been to a grocery store before. Certainly never with "Mom." *Mom* … I'm still getting used to that.

The closest thing I've ever experienced to the grocery store are the markets in Liberia. The fruits, meats, and veggies are displayed in bins or on tables. We didn't own refrigerators or freezers, so we only bought exactly what we needed for the day.

An American grocery store is wild. Have you seen these things? They are massive food stores full of bright colors. There are greeters at the door, an area where you pay to get out, and people who help you pick out what you need. I'm both overwhelmed and excited to get started shopping and finding out what this place is all about.

There are rows and rows of food at the grocery store. A million options for any kind of craving you may have are in here. I've only known of two cereals before today: Corn Flakes and Froot Loops. I'm stunned as my eyes wander down an entire aisle dedicated to just cereals. How do you pick just one box? And the fruit! It's all so pretty. It's clean, brightly colored, and organized. There are no flies or dirt like there are at the Liberian markets. I hope they have canned milk.

We pass the milk section. The cans aren't there. I already know I HATE American white milk. It makes me gag. It doesn't taste right. There's no way that stuff is really from a cow. So I just avoid milk here in America altogether. I want the canned milk we had back in Liberia. It's sugary, sweet, and reminds me of home. My brother and

I ask one of the ladies where it might be, and she points us down an aisle. *There it is! Boost!*

"Mom, we have to have this!" we shout as we place cartons in the cart. She smiles and continues to load our buggy with enough food to feed our family of seven. My mind can't comprehend that we can buy this much food at once. I watch in astonishment as the lady behind the checkout counter scans all the items. What am I going to eat first?

We load the car and drive out of the parking lot with our harvest in plastic bags filling the entire trunk. We get back to the long driveway that transports us to the picture-perfect house in the woods. There, we help *Mom* unload the groceries. Quickly, we figure out a system. *Mom* takes in her specific, personal items, and we bring the rest. This works best because we have no idea where things go.

My *brother*, Mark, keeps a few food items for himself. Good idea! You should always keep food with you because who knows when it will come again. I need to start a stash too. So I grab the bread, butter, and sardines to keep under my bed.

There are brownies on the counter. Brownies! I have the best mom in the world! She makes my sisters, brother, and me incredible things like brownies.

I probably should keep enough brownies for myself so I can eat them on my own terms. This family may work like the orphanage did. If you don't grab your own share quickly, you'll miss out. The best thing to do is to always stash what you want for a few hours later when you're hungry again. If our food supply goes down, who wouldn't mind living off brownies for a few days? Sounds like a dream to me.

I start to take the brownies I need and put them on a plate. I take most of them, but I leave enough for my brother and sisters. They'll each want one.

My mom comes back downstairs. She asks me what the brownies on the plate are for, and I tell her. "Those are my brownies." Because they are. Mine. Just in case. For later. So I can survive if (or when) conditions change. My mom lets me take two brownies but puts the rest under a glass dome as she explains that being a part of a family means sharing with everyone equally.

Enough Brownies at Jesus' Table

Having a scarcity mindset is pretty common for people coming out of poverty. We have been obsessed over making sure we don't have a lack of food (or anything else, really) for so long that our brains don't know how to not think about it. It's an actual psychological issue.

WebMD defines a scarcity mentality as being "so obsessed with what you lack that you can't seem to focus on anything else, no matter how hard you try."[2]

I can testify that this mindset genuinely takes up so much brain space that you can't think about much of anything else because you're always asking, "Do I have enough?"

This is what it means to live in survival mode.

I was almost sixteen when I was adopted. When you think about typical American teenagers, you assume that friends, fun, and their personal life take up the most space in their minds. They live out of a place of abundance, and most of them have probably never had to ask if they have enough. They have, and have always had, more than they need to get by.

My brother, Mark, and I were anything but typical American teens. We were children of war trying to find our place in a new country. We were surrounded by an overwhelming amount of stuff, but we had no way of knowing if things like housing and food could disappear again, like they had in our past.

One day, my mom went to cook pork tenderloin and couldn't find the meat in the fridge. Where was it hiding? Underneath Mark's bed, completely rotten. I know, gross! But Mark was just doing what he had always done to ensure he didn't starve. We all saved what we could for ourselves because we never knew if food would come again. Moldy pork tenderloin? Sure. An entire tray of brownies? Absolutely!

My parents did an incredible job at reassuring my brother and me that we could trade our suspicion of scarcity for assurance of abundance. I especially needed these affirmations and clearly remember my mom repeating over and over to me,

"You are loved."

"You are safe."

"You don't have a return policy."

"You're stuck with us."

"It's permanent."

"We are forever a family now."

"You are my sons."

"There is no separation here."

"You're not going to be ripped from me."

She probably felt like a broken record having to say these phrases so often through the years. But eventually, the truth did sink in. Not only because she stated these phrases so often but because our family proved they were true. They didn't ever leave me. I was safe here. We were forever family. I was a son. An actual son, in an actual family. And I was loved.

The remedy for a scarcity mindset is learning to walk in abundance. Not of stuff (or brownies) but of love, acceptance, patience, forgiveness, and being safe enough to process it all.

Jesus meant it when He said, "I have come that they may have life, and have it to the full" (John 10:10b). *The full* ... Despite even our physical circumstances, Jesus never lets us spiritually starve. He's not holding out on us or withholding anything from us.

> The remedy for a scarcity mindset is learning to walk in abundance. Not of stuff (or brownies) but of love, acceptance, patience, forgiveness, and being safe enough to process it all. >>>>

Do you ever find yourself caught up in a scarcity mindset as a child of God?

We live our lives in our comfort zones because we don't want to take risks in case there's no reward. We hoard our love and resources and keep a suspicious eye on anyone prophesying good news. We don't want to get our hopes up because what if God doesn't come through? What if Jesus decides tomorrow that He wants us to live on less?

Yet spiritual scarcity isn't possible with Christ because we live in His land of abundance. As adopted children of God, we have access to all of heaven. Yet, like the brother in the story of the prodigal son, we find ourselves yelling at our heavenly Father for holding out on us. He replies to us now just as He did to the brother then, "You are always with me, and everything I have is yours" (Luke 15:31b).

Did you notice that word? *Everything.*

All the resources of our Father's house are right at our fingertips, overflowing for eternity. While we walk around like they may run out.

Imagine now Jesus saying this to you, a parent to a dearly beloved child, just like my mom said to me. He gently grabs you by the shoulders, looks you in the eyes, and speaks over you:

> *You are loved.*
> *You are safe.*
> *You don't have a return policy.*
> *We are forever family now.*
> *You are my child.*
> *There is no separation here.*
> *You're not going to be ripped from Me.*

Hear Him proclaiming this boldly and truthfully over and over again until you begin to believe it to your core. Take a short glimpse at your past and realize that Jesus has always been proving these statements to you.

In the book of 2 Timothy in the Bible, the apostle Paul writes, "If we are faithless, he remains faithful—for he cannot deny himself" (2:13 ESV).

Even when we've doubted God's presence, wandered away from Him, or totally disbelieved and doubted, He has never faulted on who He is as a good Father. We may have allowed our circumstances to shape how we see God and ourselves, but He has never left our side, bailed, skimped on providing for us, or abandoned us. He never has and never will. Let that sink in.

Then, child of God, go and walk into your future and live the abundant, full life you were meant for.

There are always more than enough brownies at Jesus' table.

Who am I?

I'm a TerKeurst.

And we keep moving forward.

Section 5

LISTEN AND LEARN

You're off to Great Places!

Today is your day!

Your mountain is waiting.

So ... get on your way!

Dr. Seuss, *Oh, the Places You'll Go!*

Mark and I walk into the private instructor's office with Mom, and I'm excited to hear my results. You see, in Liberia, I was the top of my class. Did you know that just a few years ago I was chosen out of all my classmates to memorize and present a two-page speech to represent my graduating middle school class? I'm going to excel here in the States too. I can't wait to start school, get my driver's license, and start living the American dream.

The hope for my educational future that was inflating inside me like a bubble pops the moment the private instructor presents our American educational level. She states to my mom, in a very kind but matter-of-fact manner, that the results of our testing revealed my brother and I need to be in early elementary school.

I'm sixteen! I'm a young man who's seen war and traveled the world and, by US standards, I have the intelligence level of a child? Come on,

America! I have the ability to grow peach fuzz for facial hair. They're not going to let me sit in a kindergarten classroom.

Overwhelming disappointment settles like a rock in my gut as I realize what's really ahead of us. I can see it on my mom's face too. We have almost a decade worth of schooling to catch up on and only a few years to do it if we're going to close the vast educational gap between ourselves and our peers. How do we overcome a mountain like that?

We make plans as a family later that evening, and I learn that my brother and I are going to be homeschooled, whatever that means. Guess it's time to start our climb.

Mom has put life as she knew it on hold and taken a huge step back from ministry work to teach us. There's a group of other kids who are also homeschooled that we get to hang out with, so I'm making a lot of friends. Plus, I get to play a ton of soccer and basketball.

English is the subject I struggle with the most. Do you know how hard English is? I can recognize the letters pretty easily, but I still have a hard time comprehending what some of the words mean. If that's not hard enough already, several words are pronounced the same but have different interpretations. It's so different from the Koloqua* version of English I've heard before in Liberia. Actual American English is insane.

I study all the time and probably am getting on my mom's nerves with how many questions I ask. But I have to get out of elementary school! American high school is waiting on me.

American high school is the dream. It's got to be like the movies where everyone is from different walks of life, is free to do whatever, drives nice cars, plays sports, and there's (of course) lots of girls! I need to be a stud. I've got to start working out so those American boys don't try to pick a fight with me. Mark and I can use this time catching up to get buff.

It's not lost on me that many of you picking up this book were drawn to it because you're in the process of or considering adoption. My friend was telling me that she met a couple adopting a son with a similar story to mine. He's from a war-torn land with incredible survival instincts and yet is years behind in school.

If you fall under the adoption umbrella, I'm going to write directly to you about my schooling years before college. Why? Because I want you to know what it was like for me so that you can begin to see these educational and cultural obstacles through the eyes of your adopted child.

From the outside, my American life began to look fairly "normal." I was homeschooled through eighth grade, transferred into a private high school, then a public high school. I played soccer and basketball, ran track, and took photography courses. My soccer team even did so well that we went to the state championship.

I dated my first American girl. We wrote letters, and I'd take them to the post office, stand in line to buy stamps, mail my love note off, and wait eagerly for a week or two for a response.

Then came cell phones. When I was sixteen, I got the Razor from Cingular Wireless in the same shopping center where my dad owned a Chick-fil-A. I had a MySpace page and chatted on AOL Instant Messenger. I also carried a Walkman everywhere I went, choosing tunes from my portable CD case that was filled with all my favorite music.

We took family trips where I met my new extended family. I now had cousins, aunts, and uncles! We made a yearly camping trip to Camp of the Woods in New York. We attended church and went to youth group every Sunday. Mark and I joined Young Life. Yes, I was somewhat living a "normal" Christian, suburban, American teen life.

However, when you're adopted, life is never really "normal." You're always one foot in your new home with your other back where you used to belong. Let me pull back the curtain on what these years from high school to college were like for me.

The moment my scores came back to show that I was at a kindergarten level, my heart sank. I would have been attending ninth grade at Ocean View Christian Academy in Liberia. But here in America, they believed I wasn't any smarter than an average five-year-old.

The classes I had just come from in my homeland were filled with students from the ages of fifteen to twenty-five. The age gap was wide because of the lack of childhood education during the war. Suddenly, I had gone from sitting beside people I considered adults in Africa to being embarrassed at having to share classrooms with kids who were the same age as my youngest sister. They were babies! The process of catching up in the US educational system completely humbled me.

In school, I was made fun of for my thick accent and dark skin, even by Black Americans. They would crack jokes, saying, "I bet you're real fast because you used to chase cheetahs!" Or they'd make comments like, "I bet it feels weird wearing clothes, huh?" My peers would try to imitate my accent, which always really hurt my feelings. These experiences made me feel inferior, and I found it especially difficult to connect with other Black Americans. I didn't know their slang. To my surprise, I realized that American culture also had its own "tribes" of people. Unfortunately, though, tribes here aren't communal. They're exclusive, and you have to fit in to belong to one. Americans call them "cliques." Of course, navigating these levels of social hierarchy is not nearly as scary as running from Liberian warlords, but the emotional pain of being excluded by cliques certainly feels brutal when you're the teen on the outside.

My greatest help was my family and friends. Community is truly the best support for any adopted child. My mom homeschooled me for several years until my brother and I could catch up to a high school level of education. Then my mom, along with the other families who adopted my friends from the choir, decided to do schooling together. We all struggled, but at least we were struggling together.

Have you ever noticed how complicated the American language is?

Pair, pear, pare.

There, their, they're.

I mean, COME ON!

In the beginning, I struggled the most at fully comprehending English and the speech patterns, gestures, and mannerisms of my new country. At the beginning of high school, I was placed in a special education class for ESL (English as a second language) because my learning pace was so slow. Even when I could start to read books (like my favorite: *Tuesdays with Morrie* by Mitch Albom), I didn't understand what they meant. Communicating effectively felt like a hurdle I would never quite leap over without stumbling.

So that I wouldn't fall flat on my face, I developed eight points that would help me learn and grow enough to carry on a somewhat educational conversation with any American:

1. Listen, observe, and copy how Americans greet and interact with each other.
2. Diversify my portfolio by having friends of different races, ethnicities, and backgrounds.
3. Imitate and practice conversations by myself in private so I don't make a fool of myself in public.
4. Slowly try to practice what I've learned in one-on-one conversations with my adopted brother.
5. Watch a lot of Disney movies and TV shows.
6. Join Christian communities like Young Life, FCA, and youth group, where I feel safe enough to practice and grow.
7. Read the Bible and listen to tapes on long drives with the family.
8. Join and play on sports teams.

Once I finally made it to high school, I felt like I had been promoted. It was my first step out of the weeds. I'd spent years trying to understand the basics. Now it was time to shift into learning about true American culture.

Suddenly, school began to feel fun again. My friends taught me the coolest trends. I was picking up on slang. I loved being exposed to life with these American peers. I was learning from it all.

Want my advice?

Parents adopting children from situations like mine need to know that their children may have been through trauma and experienced hard times in their lives without the support of family and friends. They are desperate to fit in, be accepted by others, and indulge in all they have access to in America. It may be a tough road as they try to navigate an entirely new culture. So, two things:

1. **Have unending grace and understanding.** Be curious and ask questions about your child's life in their home country. Get them help to process through their traumas, learn new coping techniques, and discover what it means to be safe. Allow plenty of time and grace for them to understand the nuances of their new country.

2. **Don't make the shift too suddenly.** Celebrate your adoptive child's home culture any chance you get. It will build their confidence and make them feel more comfortable if they don't have to choose between **who they were** and **what they are expected to become**. They can love both and ease into the process of enculturation when

the family allows cultures to blend rather than separate.

If I could leave you with one tip for caring for someone newly adopted from another country, especially one that has been upended by violence and war, it's this: applaud every small win. Those tiny victories just may amount to something big.

Excelsior

"How was your day at school?" Mom asks.

"Um, I'm tired, Mom. Long day. Soccer practice. Coach *killed* us today," I reply.

"Well, I have somewhere special I want to take you. So you need to go take a shower and get ready. We're leaving in like an hour for your award ceremony," she states matter-of-factly.

Ceremony? Stunned and confused, I ask, "My *what*?"

"The school sent a letter about an award that *you* won. We have to go to an event tonight," Mom answers.

This new information baffles me. *There's no way I've won an award. My siblings are awesome at all kinds of things; I'm not really great at anything. What kind of award is this?*

"You sure it's not for Mark or one of my sisters?" I contest.

Soon, Mom and I head off to the Weddington High School academic awards ceremony, an event reserved for students who excel academically (a.k.a. not me). I'm all dressed up because I'm under the impression that this is a special occasion. As we walk into one of the large conference rooms in my high school, I take in the fancy decor and black folding chairs. Each place setting has been labeled with a nominee's name and their accompanying loved ones. I read the name tags as we walk toward our seats. I recognize these names; they're the students who are the top of our class. Names that my name does not belong next to.

"Mom, this is for smart kids!" I whine. *For goodness' sake, I'm an ESL kid who barely understands or passes classes. What in the world could we be doing here? It feels embarrassing.*

"Be patient and wait it out." My mom uses a calm but stern tone to reply so that I don't argue back. "It could be something great!"

She clearly knows something I don't, so when we finally find two aisle chairs with our names on them, I suspiciously and reluctantly take my seat. I'm racking my brain about what kind of award I could possibly be receiving at this event. Nothing. I can think of nothing that I've ever done that could be considered award-worthy. I cross my hands and just wait, confused yet excited.

Name after name is called. Every name except mine. It's been over an hour, and I'm ready to go and call it quits. Mom keeps asking me to be patient, but I'm wondering why we're even here. I knew this was ridiculous.

"The last award for tonight goes to a young man from a country called Liberia," the announcer calls out. I shoot up as if lightning struck my chair. *Me! That's me.* He begins a speech about how the awardee has outstanding character and is the most improved student out of more than two thousand students in the entire high school. "Jackson TerKeurst, you are the recipient of the administrators' Excelsior Award."

Pride swells in my chest as I accept this honor. My mom is beaming.

I go home awestruck and motivated—now more than ever—to trust God's calling on my life. I can spiritually and almost physically feel myself standing on His faithfulness. Look how far He has brought me! I can't believe it. College is in my future for sure. With Christ, I can do this.

> Who am I?
> I can't believe this, but I'm worthy of the Excelsior Award!
> I keep moving forward.

Intimidated

My biological father always had a dream of pursuing higher education. Specifically, he dreamed of obtaining a degree in business administration. In Liberia, this was a far-fetched fantasy. But now that I'm here in America, I'm expected to go to college. I can be the one to make my father's dream a reality. I can't quit now!

But can I be honest? Even though I desperately desire to attend a university, I'm intimidated to go. I have to fight the feeling that I want to just give up on school. Why? The American school system wasn't designed for immigrants like me to succeed.

I so easily can still recall thinking I was smart and being told I was on a kindergarten educational level. That sense of inadequacy and humiliation has never really faded. On top of that, I've applied to countless universities and haven't been accepted into any of them because of my low grade point average my senior year of high school.

The cold, hard facts are that I'm not smart enough and I have no idea what to study. Plus, I have so many questions. How am I going to make new friends? I don't know a soul who attends college. My biological siblings were not in school. Two of my adoptive sisters had started college but decided to take their careers in a different direction. One of them went to cosmetology school. My brother went straight into the work force. So who do I ask for advice? What do I even do when I'm there?

I'm losing hope. I feel ashamed every time anyone asks me, "Hey, Jackson! Where are you attending college this fall?" I stumble through an answer because I don't have one.

At sixteen, many American students are confidently looking toward college. They may not know where they want to go exactly or specifically know what they want to study, but at least most know that it's an option.

At sixteen, I was adopted in America and had to completely shift my thought pattern about higher education. What had been a completely far-fetched idea was now a total possibility. I could go to college!

But, to get there, I had to jump hurdles and climb mental mountains that my American peers never had to even think about. I didn't have the same documentation as everyone else. I didn't even know what grants or loans really were. Could I handle the same workload as other students while I was still trying to figure out my new culture?

Looking back on it, if I'm totally honest, I had a fear of the high calling God had on my life. I didn't want to accept that God had great things in store for me here in America. I didn't deserve any of this. Who was I to go to college? What if I failed?

In Liberia, college was reserved for geniuses only, and you could count me out of that category for sure. My mind couldn't wrap around the fact that God was opening a door for me to attend a university and that He wanted even more for me than what I had already been given. I had a home ... a family ... and now I could get a college degree.

My worst fear was that I was an imposter, a Liberian in an American disguise who would one day be found out, busted, and sent back into the war zone where I belonged.

> I had a fear of the high calling God had on my life. >>>>>

When my fears would mount, one on top of the other, I would think of my biological father. He was always a big dreamer like me and an advocate for education with a strong passion for business. His opportunity to attend school was never available due to the lack of money, resources, and reliable transportation from the village to the city.

If I wasn't going to do this for me, I was going to do it for my dad.

So I began to meet with my adoptive parents, Art and Lysa. They taught me how to apply for colleges, loans, and grants. They showed me how to choose a course workload that I could handle per semester. I'd calculate the cost of each book, meal plans, and expenses. Art would then sit down with me and go through all my findings very carefully. Other days, I spent tons of time with my mom, letting her teach me how to research college scholarships and write applications. Their support opened a door for me to take a gap year in Chick-fil-A's Impact 360 program and then go on to attend college. I stepped through that door fearfully but boldly, as if my biological dad was giving me a little Liberian shove from behind.

Americans should never take higher education for granted. It's an opportunity people a world away beg for.

Hey Jackson, Want to Go to Jackson?

"You know, Jackson," Lysa said. "There's a really good college in Jackson, Tennessee, that you will love! It's a Christian college where you will be able to get the one-on-one support you really need." She has my attention as she continues. "I have a friend who lives there who you can visit off campus or attend church with. Plus … the city has the same name as you!"

"What's the name of the college?" I ask simply, trying to hide the spark of interest in my voice.

"Union University," she states. I let the words roll over in my mind. *Union University.*

"What kind of school is that? I've never even heard of it before," I shoot back.

"Just apply, son. We'll go take a look. I think you will really like it there," she concludes.

Well, if my mom thinks so, then I do too. I apply instantly.

Golden Ticket

I'm on the edge of my seat every time the mail comes. When the truck goes by, I race out the door. Every. Single. Day. Because this could be the day that I finally find out if I get to go to college.

One day, after mowing the lawn, I decide to do my new favorite activity: take a stroll up the road to the mailbox. I open the lid, trying to stay calm. There seem to be hundreds of letters and advertisements in the mail today. *Doesn't everyone know that I have an important college acceptance letter on the way? Get a grip, people; we do not need another coupon or bill. This mailbox is reserved for one letter and one letter only: a letter written specifically for Jackson TerKeurst.*

I start to sort through the pile when I see it. A golden ticket just for me. *Am I dreaming?* Instantly, I shove all the mail under my arms and break out in a full sprint toward the house, our dogs, Champ and Chelse, on my heels.

"Mom! Look! I got a letter from that college I applied to in Tennessee," I shout through the house.

"Open it, son!" she exclaims.

You don't have to tell me twice. I open that bad boy as fast as I can. Forget the rest of the letter. I'm only scanning the document for one of two words: "rejected" or "accepted." My hands are shaking as I read, "Congratulations … blah blah blah … you have been **accepted** to further your education with us here at Union University."

Accepted? Did I read that right? Yes, accepted!

I'm speechless. My mouth is wide open.

My mom runs over and starts to hug me while screaming, "You're going to college! Guess who's going to college! My son is going to college!"

Things settle down, and I head upstairs to my room, letting the weight of this college acceptance letter sink in. I am living my father's dream.

I close the door and exhale, a soft smile of gratitude and awe spreading across my face. I *am* going to college. Falling on my knees, I give thanks to God for this opportunity. He made the impossible possible. Tears of gratitude pour from my eyes.

Who am I?

I'm Jackson.

And I'm going to college!

Prodigal

Now, with that much excitement and sincere gratitude for the opportunity, you would think that I framed my acceptance letter. You might even assume I went on to become an excellent student who tried his very best and sat in the front row of every class. Never missing a day. Always on time. Savoring each collegiate moment.

But what actually happened might shock you.

I was expelled.

That's right. As in the story of the prodigal son in Luke 15, my Father blessed me beyond measure and I basically threw it in the trash.

Attending college was like a second culture shock for me. Almost the moment I was left on campus, I began to struggle to find my identity and question who I was as a person. Looking for affirmation, I transferred my focus off my studies and onto making friends. I wanted to explore all that college really had to offer. Like a beer here or there, riding around with my friends blasting our music as loud as it would go, or taking a hit of weed by the nearest open fast-food restaurants at night.

It turns out, most universities, especially Christian ones, don't support declining grades and drug and alcohol use. You're shocked, I know.

Here's what happened …

Want to Hit It, Bro?

It took me a minute to make friends in school. I'll get to that in a second. Let's cut to the actual chase.

It was 2010, and I was a few weeks into college when I finally connected with a few guys. They broke school rules, smoked, and drank even though they were all under the legal drinking age of twenty-one. And, sadly, I joined in. I was now a part of the rule-breaking hell-raisers at a Christian college.

It may sound like I'm making excuses here, but I genuinely still didn't understand American culture well. I came straight out of a Liberian orphanage into a sheltered, well-to-do home with Christian parents. *Can you break the rules like this? Am I a sinner now? Are drinking and smoking okay? What are the boundaries?*

I was so easily influenced. I saw the open door to freedom these guys were taking, and I just followed straight behind them like a dog chasing a bone. Friends? Fun? It all looked awesome. Let's chase after it!

One night, after driving around for a bit with my friend, he pulled out a joint. "Want to hit it, bro?" he asked slyly.

"Sure," I replied. We went back to my dorm to hang out afterward, and everything was chill until ...

There's a knock at my door. I crack it open to see my resident advisor (RA) with a disgruntled look on his face. Great. I let him in.

"Someone reported you and your buddies driving around smoking something last night. Jackson, is it true?"

I'm stunned. I don't know how to answer. My mouth fills with cotton while the world starts shrinking. I realize my "friend" conveniently left his weed stash in my room the night before. That's it. We're smoked (no pun intended).

The school orders a drug test for us both, which, of course, is going to come back positive.

They expelled everyone directly involved in the incident, which included two of my friends and me, for an entire year. It was brutal. While it may not seem like a big problem compared to the horrors I had survived in Liberia as a child, this blow felt crippling at the time.

To help me learn from my actions, Art and Lysa wanted me to work to pay them back for my portion of that semester's tuition. Where was I going to live off campus? Could I find a job good enough to pay my parents back? How in the world do I get around without a car? How do I afford food?

Triggered by a sense of helplessness, I had flashbacks of being an orphan in war-torn Africa. Here I was once again, homeless and trying to figure out options with limited resources. However, this one was on me. I had to own my mistake and make it right.

And guess what? I did.

For an entire year, I rode my bike three miles, rain or shine, to and from work at Chick-fil-A. I picked up any and every shift available to make enough money to feed myself, help with rent, and save to repay my parents.

I could have been angry or bitter, blamed the school administrators, the RA, the friend who gave me the joint (and left the rest of the cannabis in my dorm room), the peer who ratted on us, or even Art and Lysa for giving me even more consequences when I'd already been expelled. Many young adults might have done just that. And, boy, did I want to! However, God had provided for me before, and I knew He would do it again.

As believers, we know that Christ gets the final word over our lives. If you read through the end of Revelation in the Bible, you know that Jesus defeats sin and death forever. So even in our darkest hour ... we are not the victims. We are the victors.

Like John 16:33 says, "I have told you these things, so that in me you may have peace. In this world you will have trouble. But take heart! I have overcome the world."

Sometimes worldly trouble isn't our fault. We are victims of war. We are in the wrong place at the wrong time. On the other hand, sometimes we cause our own disasters. We pick a fight. Do the wrong thing. Either way, by choosing Jesus, we are overcomers.

Do the hard and holy things. Make it right. Take heart.

Sometimes the hard, holy thing is letting go of the wrong people so you can surround yourself with the right ones.

That leads me to this letter ...

Dear Readers of This Book in America,

Stop overcomplicating community.

In Liberia, it's commonly understood that everyone is your brother or sister. So I walked into college believing that my new classmates would be my family. I fantasized about a wonderful group of people who would welcome me with open arms. We'd learn and grow together. Like in the orphanage, we'd be away from what we knew as home but surviving and thriving as a team.

My fantasy was quickly shattered when I walked onto campus only to realize that American people, especially college students, are incredibly individualistic. They have been raised to think that to prove themselves, they have to make it on their own. Fierce independence be praised!

When I arrived, students already had their cliques. I didn't fit in. So when I found people who accepted me, I compromised everything I had to find a "family." Even if it was with the wrong crowd, at least I belonged somewhere.

I can't be the only one who has done this. Possibly it's my cultural differences. Maybe it's just that, at my core, I'm human. You are too. So for all of us who have made the mistake of getting wrapped up in the wrong crowd, it's partly our fault, but a culture that makes forming relationships so complicated should also carry some blame.

Here are a few Liberian lessons on building community that Americans might find helpful:

1. *Instead of asking in relationships "What can this person do for me?" start asking, "What can I do to serve or benefit this person?"*

2. *Be a boundary breaker. We need others to laugh, cry, and grow with. It's human nature. As it's been said, "Build a longer table, not a higher fence."*

3. *It's okay to have a friend group, but be inclusive and open to adding people into your circle. Notice the people on the edge and pull them in.*

4. *Your community is your extended family, not just people you casually go have drinks with at the bar. If your relationships are all surface level, then you don't have true friendships. Love people well, show up in the good and the bad, and ask hard questions.*

5. *Be easy. Let people make friends with you, and make friends with others. It's simple, like the way you used to hang out with other kids on the playground. Start up a conversation, play, and enjoy life together.*

6. *Place a high value on genuinely getting to know people in your workplace, city, and neighborhood. This isn't about "climbing the ladder" or "networking." This is locking arms to make your tangible community a better place. Put more weight on an entire group of people thriving than on your own personal gain.*

I love you, America. What an honor it is to live here. Let's come together and love each other well. We could save one prodigal like me at a time just by holding space for each other to belong.

Sincerely,
Your Liberian American Brother Jackson

Back to Liberia

I was so lonely at the point in my life when I was expelled from school. It was then that I became acutely aware of the fact that I was forgetting what it felt like to feel truly connected to others, and it scared me.

After you're in America for a while, you get so used to the independence, comfort, and excess that it can make you less kind and more isolated. I needed to feel again what it was like to live in a village. I longed for the simplicity of having nothing but family and friends in my corner. I needed to remember so I wouldn't forget. I needed to go back to Liberia. So I did. Right after I received this phone call.

After a long day of work, my phone rings, and it's a number I don't recognize. I hesitate, but a little voice in the back of my mind tells me to pick up.

Is it spam? Or someone trying to use my identity? I let my questions override my gut feeling and don't answer. The number calls again. So again, I ignore it. *Geez, they're persistent. Probably a sales call.* For a third time, the number flashes across the screen. Okay, three is a lot. Hesitantly, I accept the call.

"Hel ... lo?"

"Cammué?"

"Who is this?"

"Your brother Jerry."

"Hello, brother! How can this be? I thought you were dead all these years!"

"No, brother. I made it out alive by God's protection. It was not easy. I mourned you and everyone in the family. I thought you were dead too!"

This doesn't seem real. My brother and I are talking at rapid-fire speed because we're so excited and in utter disbelief. We're now in our twenties and haven't heard each other's voices since we were just boys. We take a moment to catch up, laugh, and reminisce about the good old times we shared as children ... before the war. Then a question I'm not sure I want to know the answer to pops into my mind. "Have you seen our Papay* and O'ma*?"

"No, I have not. But I'm with our older sisters. I was able to locate them after years of searching. We're still looking for your parents. I heard your mother's sister was alive in the county next to ours. I will go searching after this call."

"What about my uncle who was captured? What about our other siblings? And Auntie Kemah?"

"They all made it out alive, but it was not easy."

Alive? They all made it out alive!

Hope, that old familiar flame, begins to rekindle again in my heart.

A couple out of Charlotte was inspired by my adoption story and had adopted two children through ACFI as a result. They were heavily involved with the organization and orphanage as board members, so when I heard that they were planning a trip back to Liberia, I reached out and asked if I could tag along. To my greatest joy, they said yes.

I start planning immediately. This will be my first visit back to Liberia since 2002, when I left my country as an orphan. Now I'll be returning as a missionary.

Life is wild!

Most of my preparations involve the usual checklist items for traveling out of the country: paperwork, updating my passport, and making sure that my medications and vaccinations are up to date. I work hard, write fundraising letters, receive support from family and friends, and save for more than a year to pay for the trip. Thrilled, I trade in my generously gifted and hard-earned cash for a golden ticket back to Liberia.

I'm going home!

I'm so excited that the phone is shaking in my hand as I scroll to my brother Jerry's number. Pacing, I wait to hear his voice again as the phone rings.

"Hello?"

"Jerry. It's me, Jackson. Guess what? I'm coming to Liberia!"

"What? No way! Call me when you get here. I want to see you."

"I will, brother. I will!"

We hang up. The next time I hear his voice, it will be when I see him in person.

We've decided to let my upcoming return be a big surprise for my family in Joe Town. This upcoming homecoming and family reunion seems too good to be true.

After flying out of Charlotte, I have been blasting Afrobeats off and on for the past twenty-four hours of travel. Finally, my music is interrupted by the voice of the pilot over the intercom. "Everyone, please fasten your seat belts. We are thirty minutes from Roberts International Airport."

Almost there! I pull down my headphones to quiet my mind as I look out the airplane window. Liberia looks so dark. *Has it always looked that dark?*

The plane lands safely on a runway filled with weeds that grow through large cracks in the pavement. The land seems forgotten. I grab my bags, push toward the exit, and am greeted by something no one who has lived in Liberia could ever forget—the familiarity of intense West African heat.

———

It's nighttime, and I'm trying to calm my soul so I can get a little bit of sleep. My internal clock is so off now, being on the other half of the world. In direct opposition to my attempts, my excitement only builds as I'm escorted by the ACFI staff to my room in their guest house. All I can think about is what familiar faces I'm about to see over the next several days as I set my bags down and slip inside the mosquito net that covers my bed.

The joy pulsing through my heart isn't going to allow sleep to come. I stay up until daybreak listening to the backdrop of my childhood—cars driving by with loud Afrobeats, chatter from people walking up and down the road, the white noise of a Liberian city. Home.

———

Today, I'm at Monrovia Home (now called Daniel Hoover Children's Village) where I spent the last months of my childhood in Liberia. Immediately, I recognize a few of the caregivers who looked after me when I was a boy, and I make a beeline for them. Dressed in their traditional West African dashiki, the women have long, embroidered tunics that flow into their skirts and to their slippers. They are always in their best dress because they take great pride in serving as Mothers, caring for children here in the orphanage.

They do so much for so many, and yet I never gave them enough credit. Now that I'm older, I can see how, when so many of us didn't have mothers of our own, they stepped up to the task. Here in the boys' dormitory, my Mother's name was Ophelia.

So clearly I remember her waking us in the morning to make sure we all went to the well to draw out water and take a bath. After she saw we were dressed perfectly in our purple and white school uniforms, she would send us down to devotions and breakfast, and then off to school. She made sure our homework was done and that we were in bed by nine o'clock. *Man, I remember breaking that rule so many times and getting in trouble with the dean.* She also helped us wash our clothes on the washing board and hang them up to dry.

Now, as I get closer to the Mothers, their smiles are just as big as I remember, and their warm hearts and arms are still open just as wide. My arms open in return, and we all embrace in a massive group hug I don't want to ever end. No one can believe this is real. I'm still laughing when we finally release our hold, and happy tears fill my eyes.

These women are heroes.

Football (a.k.a. soccer) is the universal language. We speak it well here in Liberia. This is where I learned to play the game. I carried it with me to the States, and it gave me so much common ground with other kids when I was making friends after being adopted. Now, I'm happy to be back here playing it in the African dirt, organizing and officiating a match between my new little brothers at the orphanage.

We play for hours and hours. As they run, race, and kick, I see my younger self dash down the field with the ball between my feet and a smile across my face. I am presently on the sidelines, but the ghost of my past is yelling at the memory of my brothers, my teammates. We shoot. We score!

That child of my past self and this young man of my present do a celebration dance together. Suddenly, I feel whole again, and I'm in awe of all God has done. Coming back to the moment, I'm hit with the realization that I am now the big brother.

I take a break to go see the little sisters. They are playing Lappa, and I jump right in. They giggle and want to know how a grown American boy still remembers how to play all their games. I tell them I remember because I won't allow myself to forget.

We're all tired and dusty. We have that childlike, feel-good exhaustion I've missed from sweating and playing my heart out all day. The evidence of our fun and games covers our clothes and toes and faces in a thin layer of African dust. It's time to head back to the guest house, but I'm not ready.

Vividly, I remember being in their shoes and excitedly anticipating the weeks before the missionaries would come. They would bring so much fun, Bible stories, and games. I looked up to the older boys and men who would visit so often. The saddest part was that they always left. Now it's my turn, and I don't want to cut my visit short. I don't want to be the one who leaves.

I'm sitting on the ground surrounded by an animated crowd of younger boys bombarding me with questions about America as I lift my eyes to Pastor Kofi. He reads my expression as if I outright asked him the question, *Can I please stay?* He gives me a thumbs-up. Tonight, I don't have to be the one who leaves.

* * *

"You look buff," one of the little brothers comments.

"Yeah? I work out," I brag and flex. "Let's see how strong you are!"

Several of the boys step up to have a push-up competition with me. *Let's go!*

Twenty-eight … twenty-nine … thirty … Most of the boys are falling off by now. Forty-five … forty-six … forty-seven … It's just me. I go to fifty just to prove my point. "I win!"

My American accent is slowly but surely being taken over by the Liberian dialect that I had tried to dull down over the years. Apparently, it only takes a few days for the slang and tone of your formative years to come back in full force.

"You still talk like us even though you live in America?" a little brother asks.

"Yes, of course, my pekin,"* I endearingly respond. "There are plenty of Liberians who live in the US. We have African food there as well. Cool, right? It's definitely not as good as it is here, though."

Their eyes sparkle like I'm telling them a fairy tale. Behind the shine, I see the hurt, pain, and hardship that they experience daily as African orphans in a still war-tattered country. Unfortunately, I know that look so well. It breaks my heart. My mind wanders to what I can do to help. Ideas start to bounce around in my mind, but they're suspended when the Holy Spirit whispers to me, "For now, just be present." *Okay.*

I will be fully here. I will be home.

Yesterday, after serving and building a garden for the boys and girls at the Deaf and Blind Home at ACFI, I called my brother Jerry to let him know that I'd have some free time on my hands if he wanted to drop by the orphanage. He said he'd come.

True to his word, Jerry is pulling up in an old beat-up Toyota sedan. How are the wheels even staying on that thing? I want to call it a car, but it's only barely a moving vehicle. "Thing" feels more accurate. The thing parks, and a man I think is Jerry exits the beat-up vehicle. I mean, I was seven years old the last time I saw my brother. All of a sudden, I'm not sure it's him.

As the strange man walks closer, I hear him say in a familiar, soft-spoken voice, "Cammué?" *It is my brother! It's Jerry!*

We embrace as tears fill my eyes. I hold onto him tightly, as if my grasp can prevent another war from tearing us apart. "I've missed you," I honestly confess.

He smiles and rubs the top of my head, a mannerism hinting back to our younger years that I surely recognize. "For so many years I thought you were dead. I am grateful to God for sparing your life," he replies.

Me too, bro. Me too.

We place the few gifts I had gathered in Jerry's beat-up sedan and begin to make our way to surprise everyone in the village of Joe Town, where my father was chief and many of my relatives made a home after the war. The trip would normally take about three to four hours, but based on the condition of our transportation, we're probably going to have to make a few pit stops.

In fulfillment of my prediction, we have had to fix several things that have fallen apart while en route so far. There are no mechanic shops in these parts of Liberia, so we've stepped up as pit crew to do what we can just to keep the car going. Slow and steady will have to win this race for sure. While I anticipated a few vehicle breakdowns, I didn't expect Jerry to roll to a stop for what we're encountering now.

Just ahead are soldiers standing beside a military truck with AK-47s casually strapped to their shoulders. I blink rapidly as if I can squint away this nightmare picture from my childhood coming to life before my eyes.

"Stop. Stop the car, Jerry."

"You're safe. It's good, Cammué. Trust me."

"I don't *trust*, bro. STOP THE CAR!"

"They're government soldiers. They are now the ones allowed to walk around the country with weapons. It's okay."

"It's not okay." I grab the handles of the car like I'm prepping to launch out the window to make a run for it.

"Listen, do not say a word when they approach the vehicle. Let me do all the talking. I got this."

A soldier approaches the vehicle and I physically start sweating, and not from the African heat. I'm trying to keep my cool, but anxiety is building in my chest like a bomb about to explode. I hold my breath.

"Where are you going?" the soldier guarding the street asks Jerry. "Can you step out of the car? We need to search it. Do you have a license for this vehicle? Who does this car belong to?" Every question feels like a jolt down my spine.

Jerry gets out of the car and shows his license. Everything checks out perfectly with the soldiers, but I can see that they're doing their best to find something wrong. "Do you have a few dollars on you?" Jerry leans into the car to ask me.

"Yup," I reply and pay up as quickly as possible with rattling hands.

The soldiers now satisfied, we crank the car back up (which takes a few tries) and slowly drive off.

"Whew, that was scary as heck, man!" I exhale.

Jerry gives me a look that lets me know he sympathizes with the fear still lingering in my eyes. He too lets out a long breath and then turns forward to face the road ahead.

As we approach Joe Town, I point out the different parts of the village where we grew up. After we share a few memories to kill time, Jerry asks, "How do you remember all these things? You were just a boy."

"I cherished all those moments, and I replayed them in my head over and over again. I remember because I won't allow myself to forget." I've been saying that a lot on this trip.

"I'm proud of you," he says with a wide grin.

We finally arrive and get out of the car. Immediately, my family recognizes Jerry, but I awkwardly stand beside him. No one in my flesh-and-blood family recognizes me. After many sideways glances, someone finally questions, "Who is your friend, Jerry?"

To turn on the light for everyone left in the dark, Jerry states, "That's Cammué."

A chorus of responses rise from my family: "NO WAY!" "It can't be." "Stop playing with us."

"No, it really is. It's me!" I declare through a grin wider than my cheeks.

One of my aunties, my dad's sister, comes running out of her house the moment she recognizes me. Memories of traveling with her to the market to sell our produce and following in her shadow as a boy instantly flood my mind. She was almost as close to me as my own mother. We lock eyes and, instead of running toward me, she pauses as if to take in the full sight of me. The joy that fills her heart begins to trickle down through her body and overflow in a dance. She starts clapping her hands and shuffling her feet, dancing in a circle of celebration around me. At the end of her endearing performance, she disappears into her hut and reemerges with the same smile on her face and holding her favorite rice treat. She tears off half and gives me the other, inviting me to share this "welcome home" treat. With that first sweet bite, the nervous butterflies that had been flitting around in my stomach all day melt away.

It looks as if my auntie's dance invited out the rest of the village, because neighbors are beginning to show up in the common street in traditional Kpelle tribe hospitality with enough chicken, goat, and rice to turn this family gathering into a welcome-home party just for me!

One by one, my neighbors and long-lost family members greet me and want to shake my hand. We all smile at each other but aren't quite sure what to say. Everyone's body language seems to communicate something different. Some are genuinely overjoyed, while others are faking a smile trying to hide their "I'm not sure it's really you, Cammué" expression.

While many of my family and neighbors in Joe Town still seem stunned and confused, the children evidently care much less about the logistics of who I really am. They're simply thrilled about the exotic fact that I have come here from America. Just like the scene at the orphanage yesterday, I'm again surrounded and inundated with questions from overly curious children. They ask in random order without waiting for full answers, "What is America like? Is it true that you can find money lying on the ground in the streets? Do you eat the green grass, Cammué?" (I think he means salad.) "Do they have African food? What kind of houses do people live in, and what kind of cars do they drive? Are you rich like everyone else there?"

Jerry jumps in to save me from the flood of curiosity by letting me know that my half sister from my dad's family has something to show me. She then proudly invites me into the humble but wonderful single-room hut she shares with her three children.

"You can stay with us if you don't feel like going back to the city tonight," she says.

My heart warms at her offer because she has very little space but is willing to offer anything she has to help her brother. It is so unlike the American ideal that your home has to be picture-perfect before you open your door, and it's refreshing.

"Thank you so much, sister, but I have to go back today." What I leave unspoken is that a part of me longs to stay here and catch up with my auntie and sister all night. Maybe then I could convince the rest of my family I'm real.

As if hearing my thoughts, the sun begins to make a final bow for the day, declaring that we have to start heading back before it gets dark and the road becomes more dangerous than it is already. The show is over. The moment is cut too short too soon. My family didn't even have time to really let it settle in that I'm alive because some of them didn't even come to shake my hand. They still look as if they've seen a ghost.

We all embrace and leave. As I get back in the car and stare at my long-lost family and the village I'm leaving behind, all I can think is that this can't be how our relationships end.

Glaring at the dusty road ahead, I'm hopeful but heavyhearted. I got to see my family and the celebration was nice, but this isn't exactly how I wanted it to go. I didn't expect some of them to freeze like that.

The road ahead of me is bumpy, but I have to travel down it. I have to work everything out and go back to school. I'll get the degree my dad always dreamed of, and I'll come back here to tell my family about it. I'll build a life in America so I can come here to help them rebuild their lives. The only way forward is back.

So off to America I go. But, Liberia, I'm coming back again.

"She Might Be the One, Bro"

I'm finally back at college. My trip to Liberia lit a fresh fire under me that nothing can put out. I met all requirements for reenrollment, under terms that I will be subject to drug testing at any time. *Sure, go ahead. I'm going to be as clean as a whistle.*

I'm dead set on not making the same mistakes, so I'm forming some great, healthy friendships with classmates from Haiti who have had similar experiences as me. Knowing them makes me feel way less lonely. One of my best friends is from around here, though. He's a nursing student from Memphis, Tennessee. We met in passing one day while he was heading down from the second floor of the building we both lived in. We quickly became brothers as we bonded over watching stand-up comedy videos of Dave Chappelle and swapped stories at the same table in the cafeteria. The rest is history.

"Jax, what are you doing tonight?" he asks.

I shrug my shoulders and shoot him a curious glance in response.

"Check this out, bro," he continues. "Two nurses from my class want to go out tonight. You want to come?"

"Uh, I'm not sure," I honestly reply. Nurses? I'm intrigued, of course, but I already have plans to meet a friend at the gym.

"She's definitely your type of chick," he snaps back.

I throw him a side-eye and realize his head is cocked to the side and he's lifting his eyebrows in suggestive anticipation. We both bust out laughing. *My type of chick, huh?*

"Okay, I'm in." *I'm going on a date!*

So we both get ready and then nervously make our way over to Grace 1, the girls' dorm. My roommate calls the nurses and lets them know we're in the parking lot. While we're waiting for what seems like an eternity, I see two other friends and decide to take a moment to catch up. At this rate, the girls aren't going to be ready for a while. Might as well not waste time.

Leaving my roommate to play the waiting game, I run up to my friends and chat until they have to go. We say our "see ya later's" and, as I'm making my way back to my roommate (who is still waiting, by the way), I run smack into a beautiful young woman who's headed in the same direction. No one had to tell me … I knew this was the girl I was supposed to be meeting up with tonight. We head straight toward my roommate.

"This is my boy, Jax," he introduces me casually.

"I'm Amanda," she says through a smile. We make eye contact. *Oh my gosh, I'm staring. Why am I staring? Please, stop staring.*

I'm flushed as I step away. When there's a safe distance between us, I lean over to my roommate and whisper, "She might be the one, bro."

Amanda and I share our first real date at the Red Lobster in Jackson. Pretty good spot to take a girl on a first date, right? Okay, kind of lame. I know, I know. But have you had their cheddar biscuits?

Despite the atmosphere of a chain seafood restaurant in a state that is nowhere near the ocean, Amanda and I share a truly unique connection. We have so much in common—we both love Jesus, come from humble beginnings, and seem to want the same things out of life. I speculate that she's meant for me, but I really know for sure one weekend a bit later when Amanda, her friend, and I decide to go to the local bar next to our campus to take a break from studying.

As Amanda and her friend are dancing, a guy keeps coming in way too close for their comfort.

I pull myself up to my full height, puff out my chest a bit, and yell over the music: "Bro, they're not interested. They're with me. Get lost."

He backs away instantly but then decides to make his way over again as soon as I leave. I can't believe this guy!

Fuming, I storm back over into the middle of the group and shout at him again. "The girls told you to leave them alone!"

As he leaves for the second time, he heads in the direction of the bouncer.

Not even a few minutes later, I feel a bottle hit me over the head. Blood starts pouring into my eyes as I struggle to keep my balance. Instead of helping me, the bouncer places me in a choke hold and drags me outside. *Is this really happening? It's like one of those gritty bar fight scenes I've seen in the movies.*

What does Amanda do?

Amanda doesn't cry or freak out or call 911. Nope. With the energy of a true "main character," my girl grabs a beer bottle and rushes outside to find me surrounded by a bunch of guys in the parking lot. They are determined to put me in my place, but Amanda makes it clear to all of us that she is ready to cause her own damage. Anything to set me free.

With one look at this fearless woman charging toward us with a bottle in hand and vengeance in her eyes, these bullies let me go.

Of course, Amanda and I waste no time loading up in the car and heading back to campus. There, she takes care of my injuries, just like the incredible nurse she is.

Though no more beer bottles have been involved, Amanda has been fighting for and taking care of me ever since. My hero.

Green Light

Have you read the book *Greenlights* by Matthew McConaughey? No? Me either. I listened to the audio book. You have to listen to these stories with McConaughey as the narrator. Ten out of ten! I highly recommend it.

Throughout the whole storyline, McConaughey is narrating his wild, zany life while interweaving mind-blowing life lessons along the way. When he finds an open door that takes him one step closer to his destiny, he always calls out, "Green light!"

I had lived through many yellow lights in the beginning of college, facing circumstances and relationships that slowed me down or even made me U-turn. Getting expelled had definitely been a red light screaming at me, "STOP RIGHT HERE. DO NOT GO THIS WAY."

Thank God for the red lights because they truly save our lives.

But when God gives you a green light by placing someone or something in your path that is clearly going to help you get to where He wants you to go, you'd better hit the gas. The road is wide open. This is the way!

Meeting Amanda was my "green light."

She became my rock when I didn't feel like I had anything sturdy to cling to. Her encouragement and belief in me got me through college and helped me become the man that God knew I was capable of becoming. We formed an incredible friend group and celebrated so much together throughout those college years. This was the community I had been seeking. This was a village. This was family.

I approached the end of college looking bright-eyed into the future. My identity as a college student was about to shift, but I had plans. There would be an engagement, a wedding, a real job, a home, and a family of my own in the future. I would be thrilled to one day wear the titles of husband and provider. This Liberian boy was about to get the American dream.

Green light!

Who am I?

I am about to be a college graduate.

Let's keep moving forward!

All right, all right, all right.

So Go

All right. Classes were rough today. My brain doesn't work. It's mush. My twin-sized bed could be a California king with how luxurious it seems to me at this moment. All I can think about is curling up under my sheets and, like a bear in winter, not waking again until college is over.

I pull down the sheets and slip inside. Just as I'm about to hopefully hibernate for a few months, my phone starts ringing. *Who could that be? Don't they understand I'm trying to crash?* My eyes are heavy, so I don't even open them as I clumsily reach out of the bed to my side table and blindly answer the phone.

"Hel-lo?"

"Hey, Jackson! It's Mom."

"Hey!" My eyes open and I perk up. Awake now, I continue, "Did you send me another care package?" *Yes, I hope it's a care package!*

"No, I have something more exciting to tell you. A television crew reached out to me, and they want to do a story about you. Can you make the drive to Waxhaw this weekend?"

"I'm not sure, Mom. I'm slammed. This last semester is going to kill me. Can I reschedule for next month?"

"No, this is very important. I can write your professors if you need me to."

Clearly this is a priority. And yes, Mom, save me from my professors!

"Okay, I'm in."

Upon hanging up, I grab my weekend bag and start to pack. It takes my Toyota Corolla about eight hours to drive from Jackson to Charlotte. Good thing I like driving. It's where I do my best thinking. Plus, I have two massive speakers in the trunk and tinted windows. I'm about to vibe all the way to this video shoot. Where's my blazer? Let's go!

The President's Daughter

This request is out of the blue for me, but clearly my mom has been pulling together this TV special for a while now because our entire house is video-shoot ready. Seven out of our original twelve choir members are here too—including my brother Mark—and their families are here as well. Turns out this interview is for the *Today* show on NBC. We can't believe we're about to meet current news anchor and President George W. Bush's daughter, Jenna Bush Hager. This is a huge deal! How is this even real? Oh, here she comes …

To some degree, I have already become comfortable sharing my story because I've been interviewed a few times in the past and have shared my testimony as a part of the choir and at church. As a result, many parts of my story have become rehearsed. But today I want to give Jenna a fresh approach. I can feel in my heart God asking me to be vulnerable. The call to be raw is making me feel like it's the first time sharing my story again, and I'm surprisingly nervous.

To hide my nerves, I stand up straight, ready to offer my best impression. Jenna Bush Hager is lovely with her sweet smile and emerald-green maternity dress. She's very pregnant and has that motherly glow about her. I wonder if she's having a boy or a girl. She offers me the sincerest greeting as she shakes my hand and introduces herself (as if I don't already know who she is). Her happy-go-lucky, approachable demeanor eases my nerves a bit. Our connection is instant, and I feel as if I'm talking to a friend. My nerves relax as we find seats on the couch and settle in for the interview. This conversation is going to go great! I can feel it. *Look at God move. Even though the president's daughter and I come from entirely different backgrounds, we can both sit here together united by a story of God's goodness and faithfulness. God is here using her huge platform and my nonexistent one to inspire people across the world. This moment right here is evidence of His faithfulness. He continues to make ways to share His good news, even when there seems to be none. And here I am, sitting right in the middle of it.*

I try to not let my mind dwell on the pressure as the camera rolls and Jenna begins to interview me.

"What was life like in Liberia?" Jenna asks.

"I was always scared. I was always afraid that someone was going to harm me," I reply. "But now I don't have to worry about that because I'm in a safe home and a safe country."

We smile as if we're both saying thanks to God without using words.

After a brief pause, Jenna looks at me with warmth in her eyes before she moves on to her next question. Her glance is short but long enough to set me at ease. "Tell me what the last ten years of your life have been like. How can you sum up this journey you've been on so far?"

Wow, how do I answer that? Am I tearing up? Don't cry, Jackson. The world is watching. Keep it together! "This has been the best ten years of my life so far. I'm living the dream I once dreamed of as a kid." There aren't really words to fully describe the complexity of all the blessings I have received in my last ten years, and that simple answer is as close as I can get.

"What's most important to you?" Jenna asks her last question like a big sister getting to know a little brother. Her care seems genuine, so it's easy to give her my real answer—family and food.

"Having a family. Getting to wake up every morning and not having to worry about someone shooting down my house. Or robbing me. Or doing something harmful to me. Waking up to having food in the fridge!"[1]

The interview is over, and I'm with my best friends from the choir outside on the porch in our backyard. We're chatting and laughing about how wild it is that her one-on-one interview with me and the overarching story of our choir members becoming adopted here in America is going to run in the national news when we hear my mom call for us. "Boys, can you do a few songs for Jenna?"

We look at each other and smile nervously. It's been years since we have all performed together.

"We can give it a shot," I reply.

"Oh boys, can you do the 'Mama Song'?" Lysa requests. "It's one of my favorites, and I know Jenna would love it because she's about to be a mama herself."

My brother from the choir assigns vocals and begins to count, "One ... two ... three ..." We sing, "I'm talking 'bout Mama.

Mama, we love you. Oh, Mama. We love you. Mama, we love you. From the depth of our hearts, we love you."

As we croon, Jenna, my mom, and the other families who adopted my choir brothers sway back and forth to the rhythm. Some even start to sing along as well. I'm overwhelmed with gratitude and really mean it when I sing the lyrics, "Mama, we love you."

That interview ran on NBC's *Today* show and was published on their website in May 2013. As I go back and watch, I realize that I hadn't grasped the full gravity of sitting there with Jenna.

Sitting here ten years later while I write this very unrehearsed, transparent version of my story, I see how uniquely God handpicked me for that moment. I believe a few of my choir brothers were also interviewed that day, but somehow my clip made the final cut. I got to be a voice for all Liberian children who survived the war and didn't know how to speak about what we'd been through. I got to share what it's like to be an orphan who had found a family and talk about simply appreciating that there is any food in the fridge when you wake up in the morning.

That's really what God does for all of us. He gives us stories. Stories only we can tell. But, like Moses, we have disabilities and disqualifiers. Things that threaten us to keep quiet. We look at our struggle and say what Moses said to the Lord: "I am telling you, I am not a good speaker. I have never been able to speak well. And that hasn't changed since you started talking to me. I am still not a good speaker. You know that I speak slowly and don't use the best words" (Ex. 4:10 ERV).

> That's really what God does for all of us. He gives us stories. Stories only we can tell. »»»

To our excuses, the Lord replies, "Who made a person's mouth? And who can make someone deaf or not able to speak? Who can make a person blind? Who can make a person able to see? I am the one. I am the LORD. So go. I will be with you when you speak. I will give you the words to say" (Ex. 4:11–12 ERV).

We can keep making excuse after excuse about why we can't share our story or tell others about what Jesus has done or will do. In response, God says, "So go."

Nervous about telling your testimony? So go.

Worried about everything not coming out perfect? So go.

Scared of your own pride or guilt? So go.

Debating all the complexities around how it will be received? So go.

Have a stutter, accent, or foreign dialect? So go.

Intimidated to talk to people of a different race, culture, or socioeconomic level? So go.

When we feel as if our own words may fall short, God's Word will always go the distance. We just must be bold enough to ask Him to fill our mouths with His voice to speak.

So look back at your life and then move forward by courageously sharing your own God-given story. Because when we tell of what God has done, we give hope and proof that He can do it again. That's why it's called a testimony.

Out of excuses yet? Great.

So. Go.

Graduation Day

I wake up and know that today is different.

I'm the same Jackson. I don't look any different. Or talk any different. I am the same as I was yesterday. But there will be a moment today when a diploma will be placed in my hands as evidence that I have defied all the odds. Today, a former poor Liberian orphan will become an official American college graduate.

Yes, everything is about to change. I can feel it in my bones.

My mind races in backward motion, and I'm with my Liberian dad back in his village of Joe Town again. Everything is as it was before the attacks. Kids are playing games in the African dirt. Women are cooking over fires, and people are talking in neighborly conversation throughout the village. My dad is with me by our hut. He starts to talk about the importance of education. He didn't have the chance to get schooling or pursue business like he dreamed. College was for the special, wealthy, and chosen. His eyes glaze over as he sees the life of a well-educated businessman, a life he never got to have. I follow his gaze and look back at my present self in the mirror. I'm no longer that boy listening to my dad's stories. I'm a man who is about to live my dad's wildest dreams.

Tears fill my eyes. The hot ones that you can't hold back no matter how hard you try. I would give anything for my dad to see me graduate today. He and my mom would be so proud. Prouder than anyone out there today simply because of where they came from. To them, I would be doing the impossible.

But with God all things are possible (Matt. 19:26b). I'm suddenly aware that I am face to face with a miracle.

Ceremony

The rest of the day flies by in a whirlwind of party setup, friends and family coming into town, and photos. Amanda graduated last year and has already begun her career as a nurse. She's not only stepped boldly into her career; she's also been planning this graduation party for me. With our parents knowing each other decently well by now, our families have all come here to celebrate together. There's high energy in the air, and we're all buzzing with excitement. Everyone can feel how big of a deal this is for me. I'm almost electric as I walk into the auditorium to join my classmates for our graduation ceremony.

We're graduating in the local high school auditorium and, upon entering, the space doesn't match my mood. It's old and dingy, while I feel brand new. As I take my seat, I scan the audience for my family, Amanda, and her family. I find them all in a sea of faces because they're smiling and waving at me. I make a mental note of exactly where they're located so I'll know where to look when I walk across the stage. My mind's eye catches something in the process.

My Liberian parents are here! I know I'm imagining things, but I can see them as clear as day. I can feel them here in spirit. It's as if they are sitting right there in the seats beside all the people who have loved me and taken me in. God brought them, if only through my memory, to be here for this day, and I'm overwhelmed by His kindness, that He would think of something so special just for me today. I turn back in my seat and blink back tears.

"Jackson Ter-Ter-TerKeeeerrurst?" *Really? On my graduation day you're going to mess up my name, professor?* I shrug it off because I don't really care. That's me! My name has been called, and I'm moving forward into this future as a college graduate with everything I've got. I run up to the stage, reach out to shake my professor's hand, and accept my degree. I say "thank you" way too many times to him, but he'll never know just how grateful I am. I walk to the end of the stage like an Olympian who has just won a gold medal. I look out to the crowd and beam my brightest smile toward my family. Holding my diploma, I move my tassel to the other side of my cap. Victory! I'm officially a college graduate.

Time moves in slow motion while the world cheers for all God has done for me. My family and Amanda's family aren't just shouting; they're roaring. Do I hear an air horn? In the one second that I stand here, an entire lifetime of my people's suffering flashes by. A breath and eternity are colliding as I,

The grandson of a witch doctor.

The son of a town chief.

A Liberian orphan.

A statistic of war.

A boy who was once nameless. Homeless. Barely alive …

Now hold a college degree.

Who am I?

I am my father's dream.

Thanks be to God, who keeps moving me forward.

Section 6

FAMILY

Family, well, bless your heart.
You don't choose 'em, you can't lose 'em ...
Some are crazy, some are amazing
All got a little bit of everything.

Drew Holcomb and the Neighbors, "Family"

Growing up without a true family does one of two things to you. You either become jaded and give up on being connected to people who love you, or you become hell-bent determined to create a family unit so fortified that anyone who belongs to it never has to experience the loneliness and lack of belonging that you did.

No doubt about it, I'm the latter.

You may remember that my biological Liberian parents were never married. This seemed completely normal to me until I came to America. In my culture of origin, marriage wasn't a thing. No one spoke of it, and most people didn't even know what it was. People simply lived together and had tons of children. In fact, a man could live in one place and father a child in another village, and it wouldn't be a big deal. Most of the women just considered themselves blessed to become mothers. I was the product of this scenario. My father traveled to my mother's village and got her pregnant, and about nine months later (ta-da!) … I entered the world.

While most people weren't married, there was a label for kids born of two parents who weren't solidly in a relationship. Here's what I know: nothing attacks your identity more or hurts quite like being called a "bastard child." I would never want any kids to struggle with that, especially not my own children. I want to get married and create a family the way God says to do it. I want to do this the right way. With the right girl.

Honestly, I had never even heard of "marriage" until I first came to live in the orphanage home in Monrovia. As if it were yesterday, I remember Pastor Kofi inviting all of us to a very special ceremony. Most of the town had gathered there to witness what would be the first wedding ceremony I had ever seen.

The bride looked like an angel as she floated down the aisle toward a handsome-looking man, her groom. He was clearly grown, responsible, and put together. (I noted I needed to be like him one day if I was ever going to have a bride of my own. Which I clearly now very much wanted.)

My favorite part of the entire wedding was when the preacher joyously announced, "I now pronounce you husband and wife. You may kiss the bride."

The crowd cheered like crazy as we witnessed what seemed like the kiss at the end of a fairy tale. You know, the kiss that happens right before the couple goes on to live "happily ever after."

The wedding ceremony was followed by one of the best parties I had ever been to, which I learned was called a "reception." They served tons of food, played Afrobeats, and shared nonstop celebration. I didn't quite know at that moment what exactly a wedding was, but I did have my mind made up that I wanted to one day find a bride, celebrate, and move on into our own happily ever after.

And now I know exactly who my happily ever after is—Amanda.

She's stuck by me over these college years, even knowing all the wounds from my past, and I want her there for every minute of the future. We both love God. We seem to be headed in the same direction. She's a hottie. Yes, she's the one. Amanda is exactly who I want to be my wife. So how do I do this?

Obviously, I've never proposed before. While I do recall the wedding, I can't remember ever seeing a proposal in Liberia. Here in America, people seem to go all out. Flowers. Fireworks. The whole shebang.

I think about my adoptive family. They all have such a heart for people. They make life choices based on their love for God, self-discipline, and hard work. They seem to always want to bless everyone, and they have certainly given me a model to aspire to. How would they encourage me to propose?

They would want me to propose in a way that was authentically "Jackson." Something intentional and caring … and maybe a little over the top. Because that's who I am.

So let's make a plan.

To-Do's

"Mom, I want to marry a girl just like you one day," I recall saying to my adoptive mom, Lysa.

"That means the world to me," she replied. I was and still am serious. Lysa is the woman I see as a role model for what I should look for in a wife. She runs Proverbs 31 Ministries and always seems to embody that actual verse in the Bible so beautifully:

> She is clothed with strength and dignity; she can laugh at the days to come. She speaks with wisdom, and faithful instruction is on her tongue. She watches over the affairs of her household and does not eat the bread of idleness. Her children arise and call her blessed; her husband also, and he praises her: "Many women do noble things, but you surpass them all." Charm is deceptive, and beauty is fleeting; but a woman who fears the LORD is to be praised. (Prov. 31:25–30)

Yup, that's her. My mom sets the bar really high. But Amanda definitely lives up to that standard.

I also recall my adoptive dad, Art, always saying, "You are the company you keep." If I end up as kind, genuine, and awesome as Amanda, then I'll be happy. The only piece of his advice I'm not taking is to pursue a woman who doesn't have school debt. Like most Americans, Amanda needed to take loans to pay her college tuition, but I'm not intimidated because she is responsible and has a strong work ethic. In fact, she's already working as a nurse. I'm confident we'll be able to pay off her student loans pretty quickly. However, my dad is completely against debt. He is always saying how he didn't ever want "a financial elephant to sit on top of us." While I'm not scared of elephants (I'm from Africa, for crying out loud) or the money Amanda owes, I am a little afraid to confess this to my dad.

Swallowing my fear, I man up and tell Art everything. How I feel about Amanda. How I want to get engaged. How we're going to pay off all this debt.

To my greatest relief, he doesn't look deep in thought or angry. He's smiling! I read his body language and realize he's actually excited.

"So how do I do this?" I ask.

"Well, you have to talk to her parents and make sure you get their blessing. Then talk to us. We'll plan it out," he matter-of-factly states before adding, "And we need to look for a ring."

A ring? I have no idea how to look for a ring. Shop for a ring. Buy a ring. No clue about this process whatsoever. I mentally add "look for a ring" to my list of engagement to-do's that I have no concept of how to accomplish.

Back to my proposal plan.

Should I get a ton of flowers and get down on one knee? No, too simple. What if we go on a fancy trip and I propose to her at sunset on a beach? No, that's not us either. I need to do something unique for her.

Then it hits me. A HOT AIR BALLOON!

We've talked about going on a hot air balloon ride for our five-year dating anniversary and have yet to do it. So let's do it. Let's get engaged while we're on a hot air balloon ride!

I also know nothing about hot air balloons. I mentally add "research hot air balloon rides" after "look for a ring" to my list of engagement to-do's that I still have no idea how to accomplish.

Okay, last thing. How am I going to propose to this girl while we're in the hot air balloon? What if I get a gigantic "Will You Marry Me?" sign and get all our friends to come help hold it from the ground? Yeah. Yeah. That's it!

I know nothing about getting a massive sign made. I mentally add "gigantic sign" under "research hot air balloon rides" and "look for a ring" to my ever-growing list of engagement to-do's. I'm beginning to think I may never figure out how to accomplish any of this!

I know what you're thinking. Jackson, that is A LOT for a proposal. Maybe even a bit over the top. To which I reply, "Exactly."

"A bit over the top" is who I am and have always been because Amanda deserves nothing but the best.

I speak with Amanda's dad and get their family's blessing. Then, I meet with a jeweler to find out all the crazy things there are to know about the cut and color of diamonds as I pick out a ring. I call a printing company and have the massive poster made. Also, I talk to our closest friends and convince them to come hold the sign in an open field in Chattanooga, Tennessee. Then I schedule our hot air balloon ride to fly right over that spot.

The most epic proposal in the history of ever is about to take place. I am about to start my own family. I feel so high, nothing can bring me down.

Up and Away

"Five minutes to go, Jackson," our hot air balloon guide leans over to whisper to me through his curled mustache. With his neutral-toned outdoorsman getup, he reminds me of Indiana Jones. I secretly wonder if he, like his doppelgänger, could rescue the situation if my proposal goes south.

My palms are sweating not only because I'm about to propose but also because I'm a million feet in the air in a tiny basket. Heights freak me out. I was hot and sweaty the moment Indiana Jones over there pulled out this tiny basket from the back of his van. Oh, the things we do for love!

Looking over, I see Amanda looking nervously over the edge of the basket, giving away that she is a little rocked by this experience too. It's one thing to imagine flying a few thousand feet in the air with nothing but a giant balloon keeping us afloat. It's an entirely different thing to climb into that woven basket and pray we won't come crashing to the ground. Amanda keeps grabbing onto me, which I clearly don't mind. Maybe this was a good idea after all.

There's only a minute left, and I'm starting to realize that I didn't take into account how tiny this basket would be. All three of us are standing in a four-by-five-foot bucket that shifts with every movement and midair wind gust. How in the world do I get down on one knee in here? Amanda is really shaking now. I'm starting to lose my cool. *WHAT IF SHE SAYS NO? WHAT IF WE DON'T EVEN SURVIVE THIS HOT AIR BALLOON RIDE!?*

Jackson, get it together. I breathe. Five … four … three … two … one …

"Hey, Amanda, look over here," I squeak out. She moves closer toward me in the basket and looks down to where I'm pointing. There it is. The massive sign held up by our friends and family with all my hopes and dreams displayed in one big question. I read the words aloud to her and ask, "Amanda, will you marry me?"

She isn't saying anything. She isn't trying to let go of the basket to even hug me. Nothing is happening. WHY IS NOTHING HAPPENING? Oh no. She's crying. This is bad. This is really, really bad.

Amanda can see the horror on my face and finally decides to respond. "I'm sorry, babe! These are happy tears." Her expression finally clears into a smile more beautiful than the river below us winding into the soft gold and navy hues of the Chattanooga sunset spreading across the horizon. She nods and, finally, I exhale the breath I have been holding the entire day.

Yes? She's still nodding. *Yes! Yes. This beautiful, brave, steadfast woman has just said yes! She will marry me.*

We touch down and our sign-holding friends and family rush over to congratulate us. There are hugs, laughter, and so much joy! Our guide even whips out a bottle of champagne. In that tiny basket, where was he hiding that thing? "Crack that bad boy open!" I shout.

Looking out at the celebration, I picture my Liberian family there among my loved ones. They are toasting and cheering along with us. They know this isn't just me getting engaged. This is God rewriting our family legacy. I pull Amanda in close as tears roll down my cheeks, and I feel as if I never want to let her go.

> Praise God I am a part of His family and no war,
> no loss, no thing can take that away from me.
> Praise God I was adopted into an earthly family.
> Praise God I now get to create my own family.

Who am I?
I am going to be a husband.
Praise God, who keeps moving my family forward.

Praise Party

To everyone at our proposal, this moment was a celebration. For me, it was a praise party. We had done the impossible. Amanda's "yes" set into motion God's ability to lift generational curses and break chains.

What no one knew, not even Amanda at the time, was that my Liberian mother had been cursed by witchcraft in my village when she was just a girl. The witch said my mother would never find happiness. She would have no children, and her children would never have kids of their own. Not a soul in the Gweh family would achieve anything in life. The presence of the witch was so real in our village that whenever my family and I would take the main road that led to our farms, the trees would start to shake.

My grandpa Flomo was a witch doctor who was believed to be able to reverse certain curses. He and his wife, my grandmother, fought hard against the many witches in my village to protect their children from the curses like this that had been spoken over them.

My grandmother had passed away before I was born. So, to protect me, Flomo would take me to a specific area along a village road where she had been buried. He claimed that here, "her spirit" could see us. When we would walk by, the small palm trees mixed with other tall vegetation and greenery would move back and forth, side to side with a cool breeze, as if we were by the ocean. My grandpa would always tell me not to fear. That was just my grandma being happy to see us.

> If your family placed a heavy chain on your shoulders, let me encourage you with this: You can take it off and lay that weight, that chain, at the feet of Jesus. 》》》

While witches don't commonly walk around here in America casting curses, I still see generational sin and chains restricting so many of us. I would say that a generational curse is any repeated pattern of disobedience against God that seems to separate us from receiving our fullest life in Christ. These can be things that I had to fight to overcome—an orphan spirit, scarcity mindset, and poverty. This can also be other struggles like idolatry, addiction, mental illness, etc.

God allows us to break the chains of curses when we "faithfully obey the voice of the LORD" (Deut. 28:1 ESV) and trust the Holy Spirit to "teach [us] all things and bring to [our] remembrance all that [Jesus has] said to [us]" (John 14:26 ESV).

Breaking family curses isn't for the faint of heart because it takes hard work and daily obedience to God. Some curses aren't broken overnight. But if we're willing to use God's truth to chip away at the chain of lies Satan has been welding together, we can eventually break free of all that kept our ancestors captive.

If your family placed a heavy chain on your shoulders, let me encourage you with this: You can take it off and lay that weight, that chain, at the feet of Jesus. You weren't meant to bear it, and He can carry it. Small steps of surrender and obedience on His narrow path will always take you, and your family, in the right direction— toward freedom.

Let's Get Married

It's a perfect bluebird fall morning as I sip my coffee on the balcony of my hotel in downtown Knoxville, Tennessee. I'm up early because there's no way I could sleep in. This is October 29, 2016, a date I'll remember for the rest of my life. It's my wedding day!

Staring off in the distance, I exhale into a broad grin as I reflect on all God has done and is about to do. A village boy from the jungle of Liberia who was once teetering on the edge of death is about to step into a new life where I'm worthy of love as a husband. Yes. A husband. I like the sound of that. Like my view from this hotel balcony, I too feel on top of the world.

Our wedding planner has the day clocked down to the minute. In just a few minutes, we're scheduled to head to the venue in my Nissan 350 Z Coupe. Every Liberian boy dreams of having a super-fast car, and here I am about to slide into my sleek, silver two-door coupe with my bride-to-be. What a world I live in! I sing my blessings to the background music of a revved engine.

⸻

Walking toward the pavilion under an open sky, I head toward the end of the aisle at Dara's Garden in Knoxville. With twenty acres of land, a stunning historic home, twinkling lights, and fresh flowers, our venue looks like the setting for a fairy tale. Everything feels like a dream. In traditional wedding fashion, our pastor stands behind me and my six groomsmen flank my left side. A smile curves from my mouth out of sheer joy as my eyes rest on these incredible men who choose to stand by me. I then turn toward the hundreds of people sitting in the white chairs in front of us. *All of these people are here for Amanda and me? This is really happening? We're getting married!*

My stomach somersaults as my brain begins to turn over thought after anxious thought. My mind flips in a direction I didn't expect. *What if Amanda is making a big mistake? What if I'm the worst husband? What if my fears and trauma and past can't carry us into the future?*

My knees start to wobble, and I remember to unlock them. I've heard way too many stories of people passing out, and I'm not about to be another statistic. I start shaking my legs to get the blood flowing back through my body. *Oh gah! What if this doesn't work and I black out at my own wedding ceremony?* My doomsday thinking is interrupted by a change in the music. The atmosphere shifts. My mind stops spinning and goes silent because there she is, my beautiful bride, walking down the aisle.

All eyes are on Amanda, as they should be. Who could miss her? She's stunning in a white strapless lace dress. Her hair is tucked to the side in an elegant bun. She holds a bouquet of lavender with deep purple, blush, and cream flowers. She is heaven.

For a moment, I'm remembering the Liberian wedding I attended as a child and the way I dreamed I'd one day have an angel-bride floating toward me, the groom. I am now the man at the end of the aisle, and Amanda is my angel. As her father gives her away and her hand slips into mine, I'm keenly aware of the transfer of power that has just occurred. Her dad has entrusted me with the gift of his daughter. I squeeze her hand. It's as light as a feather yet carries so much weight.

"Dear family and friends, welcome to the celebration of the love story of Amanda and Jackson," the pastor begins. "A love story that began not just a few years ago but before the beginning of time. You see, when God writes your love story, the first heartbeat, the first burst of passion, the first sense of longing for someone is actually for Him."

I'm clinging to the knowledge that this is truly all for God. It's the only thing keeping me grounded as we go through the motions of the ceremony. I'm here but I'm not, as nervous energy and a sense of surrealism takes over. We are guided to a small white cross on a table where Amanda and I, still hand in hand, bow our heads as we're prayed over. The pastor's words flow from speaking to the crowd to addressing God on our behalf in a prophetic blessing.

"I pray Your hand of guidance and anointing be on Jackson as he leads this home that You've brought together. I pray Your Holy Spirit continually fills him, God. May You lead them to do amazing things together for Your kingdom. I pray for Amanda, this tender heart that You've formed to make a difference in others' lives for Your glory. Guide them to make a difference in the generations around them. In Christ's name, I pray. Amen."

Rings and vows are exchanged. We are declared husband and wife. We will make a difference. I exhale.

Yes and amen.

Can I kiss the bride now?

Imagine you're at a fancy restaurant. Your friends have been talking this place up to you for a while. You're pumped, and expectations are high. Like, you're thinking this is probably going to be one of the top dining experiences of your life. You get dressed up, sit down with your friends, and order the best thing on the menu. Let's say it's lobster.

The steaming lobster comes out to the table. All your friends "ooh" and "aah" as the waiter sets it down before you. It smells great. There are pats of butter and beautiful garnish. No denying, it looks fantastic. Salivating, you dig in.

You're expecting exquisite, but something is ... off. You can't put your finger on it, but this dish, as beautiful and perfect looking as it is, seems not quite right. You call the waiter back over. He understands. After all, this is a top-of-the-line restaurant. The food should be perfect. He whisks it back to the kitchen only to return and let you know that the chef is sorry. He forgot to add a key ingredient—salt.

That's the off taste that was left in my mouth the moment I notice my parents having a private meeting in another room during our celebration. My paternal grandparents were praying with their hands over Lysa and Art. On the outside they seemed perfect. They were dressed to the nines. In public, they were the picture of a wonderful marriage. They were the couple so many aspired to be like. But there, in that room, their faces were solemn, maybe even a little angry. This was my wedding day, so solemn anger wasn't exactly what we were serving up. Everything was supposed to be so good and happy, with everyone enjoying the best experience possible.

But a key ingredient was clearly missing between them. Something was just a little ... off.

Throughout the reception, in a tent bursting with people, celebration, food, and dancing, that "off" feeling tugged on the edges of my mind. Like a dull ache, I couldn't shake it. So I talked to my family just after getting back from my honeymoon.

I was shocked at what I learned. Something is going on between my parents. Dad is in a really dark place, seeking intense counseling and not living at our house right now.

I'm swallowing all the details, but my brain is screaming, *NOT MY DAD!*

My dad cannot leave.
When dads leave, they don't come back.

———————

For a moment, I'm that small boy back in a Liberian village help-lessly watching as my father is stolen away. It's been mere seconds since the soldiers have taken over, and apparently that's all the time that's needed to completely destroy someone's life. They shove my beaten father in the truck and drive off. I am now an orphan. I blink.

I'm back in the orphanage trying to remember my name, my identity, just enough to write it down on a piece of paper. I'm strug-gling. I can't remember. There's a block in my brain. As if to survive, I didn't even exist before the war. Someone else chooses my name, my destiny, for me. Once again, I am Jackson the Orphan. I blink.

Except this time the picture in front of me doesn't change. While I'm just starting to build my family with Amanda, my adoptive fam-ily is falling apart. I'm caught yet again in a crossfire, but this time it's not soldiers attacking us but rather circumstances and life deci-sions. Something tells me this is going to be just as life shattering.

Where do I run this time? If I'm really a resident of heaven like the Bible says, if I'm really able to break generational curses, then why does it so often seem like I keep walking back through hell? Even when we live obediently, serving God and making selfless choices again and again, the enemy attacks. So how will I survive this time?

Don't Avoid the Void

You're thinking what I was thinking. *This is bad. This is really, really bad.* Well, when it rains it pours, right? Just when we believed this couldn't get any worse, Amanda also found out that her parents were walking through marital issues and decided to separate. They had been living in the same house until we got married but were secretly struggling. Our entire world was falling apart while we were putting our lives together.

Amanda will tell you that it all hit me way harder than it hit her. And she would be right.

I had watched my birth family be destroyed by war. I didn't even know if my parents or siblings were alive for years. Why would any family in their right mind *choose* separation? I knew firsthand that it was miserable and terrible to be without family. To me, family was the greatest gift imaginable because it seemed like such an elusive, powerful thing to be a part of. To me, family was a treasure that had been stolen from me and returned in a different package, only to then be stomped on.

You see, I had this vision that my adopted family would become an incredible team. Then, my wife and I would get married, and we'd join forces with my already awesome family. We'd get to create this big, beautiful, and strong unit. Now, my hopes of creating the dream team had, because of divorce, turned into a nightmare.

But I'm not alone in this. So many of us are walking through really hard family issues. According to the American Psychological Association, approximately 40–50 percent of first marriages end in divorce, and more than 8.3 million divorces have happened here in the US since 2000.[1] That means that around half of you reading this book in the States have been impacted by your family unit falling apart. Some of you, like me, may have been disconnected from your birth parents and then watched your adoptive parents' marriage also deteriorate. It's a double whammy and rough on us all.

Family, especially our family of origin, is a huge source of our identity and security. For those of us from collectivist cultures that prioritize group desires and needs over the individual, family is genuinely everything—even more so than our community, village, or tribe.

Transparently, I was trying to fill the hole that losing my birth parents had left by bonding with my adoptive ones. Like a sinkhole opening in the earth, the surface of my internal world also started to break down. Again, the massive gap in my heart caused by loss, grief, mourning, and trauma was exposed.

Here's the best advice I'll give you when you can't find identity in your family unit—don't avoid the void.

You've maybe heard it said before that there's a "Jesus-size hole in your heart." I'm a living testimony to the fact that it's true. When you try to stuff that hole with a substitute, it doesn't work. It's as if the hole widens around it. I think it's because Jesus is the concrete that fills the void and provides us a solid foundation to stand on. He bridges the gaps in our lives and never breaks apart. Our identity as children of God is what grounds us.

God as a father is consistent, never changing, and He doesn't leave. In Psalm 18:2, the author David confirms this by declaring, "The LORD is my *rock*, my *fortress* and my deliverer ... in whom I take *refuge*, my shield and the horn of my salvation, my *stronghold*."

Yes, Jesus is concrete. A firm foundation. A good Father who always claims us as His children. Everything else is just counterfeit and won't be able to support the weight of life. Families fall apart; Jesus doesn't.

When we try to fill the voids in our lives with a substitute for Jesus (even with something as seemingly permanent as family) and circumstances cause our counterfeit to collapse, we end up trying to tiptoe around the fact that we've lost our identity. We hop around in life pretending like we know our purpose and are confident in our placement. We walk through our days hoping no one will notice the gaping hole in our heart.

To be straight up with you: If we avoid the void instead of filling that gap with Jesus, eventually we fall in.

I know I did. I fell hard.

———

Hope is lost. *Who even am I? I'm a hamster on a wheel of negative thoughts, and I can't get off. Maybe we shouldn't have even gotten married. If I'm a product of a biological mom and dad who couldn't even get married and an adoptive family that was being torn apart, what makes me think Amanda and I can make marriage work?*

I know it's a bad spot to be in, but I mentally don't move. I'm planted in an emotional storm cloud and letting it envelop me. This is a very gray "woe is me" feeling that probably started to hover over my head years ago.

I'm going to figure out where this started. Maybe when we were setting the wedding date. It's hard being an adopted son with sisters as incredible as mine. They are successful. Beautiful. And the true blood of my parents. When they got engaged around the same time as Amanda and me, we had to debate over who would get which wedding date. Everyone had to be flexible. No one got the exact date they wanted. After all, three siblings were getting married months apart in three different states. Amanda and I came excitedly to the family with a May wedding date and got asked to consider late summer or early fall instead. My anxiety kicked in, and I struggled to agree because it didn't seem fair. But families have to compromise. What choice did we have?

No. Back up. It wasn't the wedding planning. Maybe it was dating. Being a Black boy from Liberia with two White parents and three White sisters trying to date a White girl in the south was (shoot—it still is!) creating quite the interesting dynamic within our surrounding community. I was always striving for acceptance and approval. I'm beginning to think I'll just always be wrestling. Always be striving.

Amanda and I have just jumped into the fighting ring for our marriage and the life God wants for us, and I already feel punched in the gut.

Who am I?

I'm not sure.

I'm married and making it.

I'm knocked down but not out.

Not yet.

I keep moving forward.

When Our Private Problem Becomes Public

We are not here to talk about my parents' divorce. We're here to talk about what it's like being an adopted kid who loses their birth family and then sees their adopted parents divorce and how we can love those children well through the process. So all you need to know for my story is this: My dad made some choices none of us thought he would ever make. Though my mom forgave him many times, my parents ultimately had to face the reality that divorce was the only option.

To be clear, both my parents loved me well through this process and really did their very best for all their kids to stay healthy and happy. So while I'll keep the details of that scenario super short, I don't want to gloss over my experience as a result of my parents' separation.

The resulting anxiety was crippling. Normally I'm a pretty happy-go-lucky guy. However, due to my past, or just my personality, I like to keep all the precious emotions and deeper thoughts to myself. The divorce made me want to go hide in a spiritual bunker until it was all over. But I couldn't hide away from the world. As if I were standing in the middle of this battlefield naked, I felt so exposed because everyone could see our hurt and desperate need for healing. It hurt, and I had to watch every member of my family suffer ... again. So I didn't want to go outside and face the barrage of questions and statements like, "Aw, Jackson, I'm so sorry to hear about your family." Yeah. Thanks, lady. Me too.

In an effort to avoid the pain, I tried to develop a battle strategy of anticipating the public hits and wounding words. I once again began living in fight-or-flight mode because I didn't know if the right thing to do was to stand up for my family or run away entirely. I was paralyzed in the middle ground. Once again, I was a little boy hiding in the woods watching his parents get beaten and burned, not knowing where or who to turn to for safety.

Again, both seeking refuge from the war, I found my brother Mark. We seemed to be each other's last man standing. We both knew men were capable of incredible evils. We had seen them murder, rape, torch villages, tear families apart, and commit unmentionable acts of violence. Some of these men, because they were captured by rebel armies, were forced into these atrocious acts. Their only options were to kill for their captive armies or be killed by them. What made no sense to us was why, when given so much freedom, peace, and provision, anyone would *choose* to rip apart their own family unit. When given the option, why in the world would anyone create their own war?

Victory Over the Void

I knew that if I were to claim victory over the void, I needed to do two things.

One, trust God.

Two, find my identity first and foremost as His child.

I had learned the hard way that the ground can break apart right under our feet, but if we are standing firm in Christ, the void won't swallow us whole. "Jesus Christ is the same yesterday, today, and forever" (Heb. 13:8 NKJV). Life changes, God doesn't.

By the time I finally learned to live authentically and gain victory over the void, I had gained several life lessons:

1. Authentic conversations transform relationships (even in traumatic situations).

> If one member suffers, all suffer together. (1 Cor. 12:26a ESV)

Hardship can do one of two things in all relationships. It can bring us closer together or drive us further apart. When my family and I started having real conversations about all the struggles going on in our lives, I also began to have raw conversations with Amanda. It took time, but we learned to identify our feelings in healthy ways. Once I removed my protective armor and invited her into the dark spaces, I opened the door for her to come in and hold a light.

If we really want to transform our hardship into an opportunity for growth and healing, then it's important that we learn to communicate openly, honestly, and without walls. By being emotionally real and transparent, we can hold the pain together and heal together. After all, we're already suffering together.

2. Trusting God's timing looks like handing Him your hustle.

> Many are the plans in a person's heart, but it is the
> LORD's purpose that prevails. (Prov. 19:21)

My fifth-grade teacher in Liberia used to always quote this verse to us by paraphrasing, "Man can make his own plans, but God always has the last word." Isn't it funny how we receive Bible verses or themed conversations throughout our lives that seem random until one day, like a puzzle, all the random pieces come together and begin to make sense? It's as if God's been trying to say something specific this whole time, but it takes a while for us to finally understand the message.

Along our path, He's been placing all the encouragement we need to make it through. He equips us before He calls us because He sees the big picture. He has a plan. He gets the final word. Even when that plan or word is different than we want it to be.

Prior to watching my second family fall apart, I had been living as a habitual "hustler." If things didn't happen on my time, I would get frustrated and anxious. The humbling that I received during this season was the reality check I desperately needed—we are human BEINGS. Not human DOINGS.

We can only do what God has given us the power to do. So the best stance we can take in life is to trust in His promise that He'll use our gifts to accomplish His holy purpose.

All of us are limited people who are loved by a limitless God. We can make plans and work hard, but then we have to surrender control and trust that God will bring us right where we're meant to be. He'll fill the void with His grace. All we have to do is accept it.

3. Being patient requires being present.

> But the fruit of the Spirit is love, joy, peace, patience, kindness, goodness, faithfulness, gentleness, self-control. (Gal. 5:22–23a ESV)

It's always a little wild to me that it's the "fruit" of the Spirit and not "fruits" in plural. As if, when we're connected to the Holy Spirit, we start producing love, joy, peace, patience, kindness, goodness, faithfulness, gentleness, and self-control. The fruit of the Spirit seems to be a complete package, not a pick-and-choose from the fruit stand.

Like a limb that's been snapped but not broken from its tree, I've always felt like my "patience" branch was a little broken. While my anxiety has been flourishing, my patience has dwindled. Often, I've wanted quick solutions more than an eternal Savior.

So when I couldn't fix my parents' problems, I did the only thing I could do. I waited.

I waited for them to work it out. Waited for my wife to hold me and hear me. Waited for answered prayer.

I waited. Waited. Waited. And during that season of waiting, I learned that when I became future focused, I became anxious. I disconnected the moment from the Holy Spirit and tried to connect it to my own power to fix the problem. This only produced a ton of anxiety because, on my own, I didn't have the power to heal or solve anything. However, when I chose to do the hard but holy work of remaining present and asking God to show up in the middle, it felt like the Gardener was wrapping a piece of mending tape around my "patience" branch.

Little by little, I felt my connection to Christ in that area become stronger. And wouldn't ya know it? I started to produce the fruit of patience.

If we want to wait well, we need to connect to the Spirit. He's in the middle of any problem, not just on the other side of it. Being present will produce the patience we need to see it through.

4. Pursue relationships with people who will hold up your arms when you're tired.

> When Moses' hands grew tired, they took a stone and put it under him and he sat on it. Aaron and Hur held his hands up—one on one side, one on the other—so that his hands remained steady till sunset. (Ex. 17:12)

I believe Aaron and Hur are the unsung heroes of Israel's battle with the Amalekites. While Moses held up his arms, the Israelites were winning. When he'd put his arms down, the Amalekites would start to take the victory. So Moses got stuck holding his arms up in the air. But Moses, like any man, grew tired. That's when his bros Aaron and Hur stepped in. When Moses could no longer do what God had called him to do, Aaron and Hur held his arms up. When he needed rest, they gave him a chair.

We all need friends like Aaron and Hur. Especially in seasons that drain us. When we're trying to avoid the void, we need someone in our lives who faces it with us, someone who holds us up when we're too tired to fight the battle alone, and someone who truly wants us to win.

Surrounding myself with people, especially men (like Aaron and Hur) was the wisest thing I think I did during this challenging season. Thankfully, I was able to rely on genuine relationships with people who lifted me up. They were strong enough on their own to help hold up my weighty circumstance, knowing one day I could return the favor when I was healed and they were weak. This community reached out to me when I fell into the void, and together, they pulled me out of the darkness.

What I'm about to say might be a bold statement but ... it's possible that watching my parents' relationship fall apart actually saved my own marriage.

Out of observing what made their connection fall apart, I learned what might keep a marriage together. I learned some important actions that could repair relationships.

One, I learned how important it is to keep trying, even when it doesn't seem like there's hope. I learned to do the internal work at an individual level so I could simultaneously grow with Amanda as a couple. I learned that I needed to understand my spouse's specific needs and love language so I could serve her well. I also learned to forgive quickly, be patient, and offer a ton of grace.

Two, I became painfully aware that nothing is ever actually stable or secure except Jesus. So Amanda and I were going to be tested a lot in our marriage too. We had to predetermine the answers to these questions: When Satan tries to divide us, how will we handle it? Are we going to give up too or fight for the family we want? When our family system is shaken, do we really want to pass the weight of divorce and separation down to our kids and possibly even our grandchildren and great-grandchildren? Or will

I step up and become the man I always needed to lead our family into unity?

Perhaps most importantly, I learned that we can view everything as a lesson. Even when facing the most painful situations in life, we need to be willing to learn from them so we can leave the void stronger, wiser, and better equipped for the battles ahead.

Truth is, back in Liberia, when I was trying to survive the war, I could have chosen to become a child soldier. It would have been the easy way out. There was some security in it, like weapons, food, and shelter. Or I could have given up on life and died beside one of those trash piles at the orphanage. Choosing to live was not easy. My situation was beyond painful and miserable, and escaping the torture of starvation seemed more appealing than I want to admit.

> Even when facing the most painful situations in life, we need to be willing to learn from them so we can leave the void stronger, wiser, and better equipped for the battles ahead. 〉〉〉〉

During the divorce, I could have decided to give up on marriage because it's really freaking hard. I'm not saying my parents didn't fight for their marriage. They did the hardest thing by deciding to lock arms and try to heal. I'm speaking for me personally. I could have quit while Amanda and I were still early in our marriage to avoid all the hard that may come later.

However, I've always chosen to do hard things because what I've learned is that often, when we choose what's easy in the moment, we're actually choosing hard later. Becoming a child soldier might have given me food in the moment, but it likely would have also led to mental and physical torture down the road. Giving in to death would have ended my immediate suffering, but it also would have meant giving up on all the life I still had yet to live. Letting go of my hope for a successful marriage would have been an easy way to stop thinking about the painful dissolution of my adopted family, but it would have also meant seeing the family I've always felt called to create slip right through my fingers.

I've learned not to take the easy road, which means I have learned to choose the narrow way. We are incredibly capable of doing hard things, so I'll keep choosing hard things. What about you? What will you choose?

Section 7

HOW TO LOOK BACK TO GO FORWARD

Visually and symbolically "Sankofa" is expressed as a mythic bird that flies forward while looking backward with an egg (symbolizing the future) in its mouth ... "Sankofa" teaches us that we must go back to our roots in order to move forward. That is, we should reach back and gather the best of what our past has to teach us, so that we can achieve our full potential as we move forward. Whatever we have lost, forgotten, forgone or been stripped of, can be reclaimed, revived, preserved and perpetuated.

Western Regional Council of Black American Affairs

Ironically enough, I learned in depth about the Sankofa bird after I started to write this book. In a meeting about the proposal, I was asked if I knew about the symbolism around the African mythical creature. I smirked because my wife actually has the bird as a tattoo. Amanda introduced me to it when she was searching for an image that would represent her growth from her past.

The moment the bird was brought up, I started to connect the dots between my book and what Amanda had taught me. The Sankofa bird almost directly embodies the concept of "the only way forward is back." Its origins are linked back to the people of Ghana (another West African country near Liberia), and its name directly translated is SAN (return) KO (go) FA (look/seek/take). The Sankofa bird embodies the phrase: "It is not taboo to fetch what is at risk of being left behind."[1]

Maybe my fellow West Africans were on to something because we seem to be on the same ancient page here.

The Bible says some really incredible things too about looking at what God has done in the past in order to move confidently into the future. We often can figure out where we're going by knowing where we've been. We recall what God has done for us before to trust that He will come through again. To really step forward with the prize egg (our hope and future) we have to answer His overwhelming call to do this one thing: remember.

> **Remember** the days of old; consider the generations long past. Ask your father and he will tell you, your elders, and they will explain to you. (Deut. 32:7)

> **Remember** the word that Moses the servant of the
> LORD commanded you. (Josh. 1:13a ESV)

> **Remember** the former things long past, for I am
> God, and there is no other. (Isa. 46:9a NASB)

> Do this in **remembrance** of me. (Luke 22:19b)

> Therefore, **remember** from where you have fallen,
> and repent, and do the deeds you did at first. (Rev.
> 2:5a NASB)

A verse I'm particularly connected to as a mission statement for this book is this:

> But I have written very boldly to you on some
> points so as to remind you again, because of the
> grace that was given to me from God. (Rom. 15:15
> NASB)

Now, I didn't go through my Bible and count, but the Biblical Stewardship Resource Library says that the word *remember* is used more than 1,200 times in the Bible.[2] That's A LOT of moving forward by looking back.

But looking back takes courage.

Truth Tornado

Have you seen *Frozen II*? As I was telling a friend's kids about this portion of the book, they shared a scene from this movie where, on their epic quest to uncover the truth of the past to save the future of their kingdom of Arendelle, all the main characters are swept up in an enchanted forest by a tornado. While they're hurling through the air, Elsa uses her powers, which are ice blasts that shoot from her hands (cool?), to try to get out of the wind. Instead of breaking up the tornado, the wind begins to form visions of the past in the form of snowy ghosts. Elsa watches the ancient reels from inside the storm. These frozen-in-time scenes form a foundation for the truth she seeks that ultimately will save her people, family, and self.[3]

Disney, this has some serious depth to it!

Let's follow Elsa "into the unknown" because in order to move forward, we're going to have to allow ourselves to be swept up at times into the storms of our past. While there are memories we wish we could forget, they are not scenes we can just cut out of the story of our lives. Each moment has made us who we are and, if we want to embrace all that God has formed us to be, we have to trace His hand over our lives. Even in the places He has seemed absent. Even in the darkness where we were desperately wondering if He really was the Light.

We have to go back to look for Him in order to discover the truth of our identity. Only then will we know how to help others ... and ourselves.

If you've tried to throw out scenes from your story because you've been through trauma or they are tainted by deep shame, regret, or pain, then chances are you're a bit lost like I was (and still am at times). There were so many things I tried to forget about my past because facing those memories was scary and painful. I'd witnessed far too many brutal experiences, truly horrific scenes I wish I could unsee. But as I ran from my traumatic past, I got lost along the way. I had been blocking out entire segments of my life because I was too afraid to face them. As a result, I didn't understand my full cultural, personal, or spiritual identity. Those gaps in my story now stood as obstacles I needed to cross.

I was stuck.

What I found was that, if we pull out clips of our life, Satan will try to fill in his own version of a script for our memories. He'll slip in negative emotions to compound our hurt. He'll write over God's Word with lies like these:

> "You're abandoned, an orphan; no one loves you."
> "You're forgotten, so your life is meaningless."
> "Look at all the bad stuff in your life. Why trust
>   in God to be good?"

If we want to get unstuck and move forward, if we want to take back the scenes of our life the Enemy has stolen, then we've got to look at all the ways God has woven the good and bad sections of our lives into a stunning story of redemption and grace.

We have to bravely jump, like Elsa, into the truth tornado and allow our mind and body to swirl through the memories to discover the miracles. Only then can we walk through the old pain to find new healing. Only then can we confront our curses—the lies that have been spoken over us—so we can be set free.

> We have to go back to look
> for Him in order to discover
> the truth of our identity.
> Only then will we know
> how to help others ...
> and ourselves.   »»»

The Bible calls us to **remember**. Recall all that God has done in our lives and in the lives of others. And then, with Christ, walk on. The only way forward is back.

But looking back takes work.

The Work Is Worth It

"Clarity is always a conversation away," my adoptive dad, Art, used to say. Despite some of his mistakes, Art was always a great man to me. He offered me so much wisdom and insight. Statements like this one stick with me still today. He was absolutely right—if we want clarity about where we're headed in the future, we need to have a healing and hopeful conversation about our past with ourselves and with those we love.

If you're an orphaned, adopted, or fostered child with trauma in your background, or you're parenting a child who falls into these categories, I want to equip you with some tools that might help you start these conversations about the past.

Seek Counsel

Proverbs 24:6 says, "For by wise guidance you can wage your war, and in abundance of counselors there is victory" (ESV). It's really a battle tactic from the Devil for us to fear our past. If he can keep us trapped in past pain, then we never fully heal and we lose all hope for the future.

The Enemy hopes that we'll remain forever crippled. That way, we will walk with wounds onto the spiritual battlefield of life. If we think we're too weak to be a threat, then he gains terrain as he seeks earthly dominance. If we want to wage war and fight back against Satan, then we must seek "wise guidance" and rely on an "abundance of counselors."

That's why, when I got to this section of the book, I knew I needed to sit down with my friend Darin Short, a trauma-informed therapist and the director of Forest Hill Counseling. As I picked his brain regarding advice for parents wanting to adopt or foster, we dove first into the topic of trauma and children. He differentiated two types of trauma: traumatic events and embedded trauma.

> **Traumatic Events** (identified in professional circles as type one trauma) include any experience that feels like a life-or-death situation. These moments feel incredibly scary and may include one-time events like a car wreck, a house fire, or a physical injury. For an adopted or fostered child, this traumatic event could be the day their parents left them. It typically involves very real and perceived horror and terror.

> **Embedded Trauma** (identified in professional circles as type two trauma) is connected to social structure and is created by repeated events in a relational system. This type of trauma interrupts a child's ability to trust and typically makes them feel skeptical or detached. Some examples would be harsh words continually spoken over them such as, "You'll never amount to anything," "No one will love you if …," etc. It could also be something physical like repeated sexual abuse.

If we're looking at my life story, I have to examine the traumatic moment in Liberia when I was raped by a woman who was supposed to be watching me while my dad was visiting a neighboring town. I trusted my dad and, therefore, I trusted this woman. In return, she stole my purity at around six years old, and I have still, even as an adult, never been able to forget that traumatic event. It will forever be burned into my memory.

Equally as bad was that, as a result of my position in the social structure, I felt like I couldn't tell anyone. I couldn't be a snitch. This was a traumatic event with elements of embedded trauma because the level of trauma in my experience was compounded by my culture.

By denying my ability to seek help, healing, or justice, our cultural system caused ongoing "second wounds" that added complex layers to my original injury.

This led me to ask Darin exactly what parents should know regarding caring for a fostered or adopted child who may have similar memories or experiences in their past. He pointed me in a direction I didn't expect to go.

He didn't start with how to help the child. Instead he said, "Parents have to go back to their own story if they want to move forward with their kids." If parents have unresolved trauma or aren't comfortable with their own past, they can actually compound their child's present trauma by negatively reacting to it. For example, if a parent had abuse in their past but didn't heal, they can be triggered if their kid brings up their own abuse. Instead of having a helpful conversation, the parent lashes out or shuts down. The harsh reality is that parents can't truly help kids regulate if they're disrupted too.

"What all children need is a secure base and sense of safety to help them regulate when they can't regulate themselves. Kids carry trauma in their body, as we all do. Coregulation can't happen if their parents or caregivers aren't secure," Darin stated. "So the big question for parents wanting to adopt or foster is … **Are you willing to begin to engage your own story so you can help your child cope with their past and present?**"

Darin also recommends that parents should learn to master six key skills as identified by clinical social worker and counseling expert Adam Young. The BIG SIX every child needs from their parents include:

1. **Attunement:** Parents should be attuned to their child's emotional needs.
2. **Responsiveness:** When kids are distressed, they need parents to respond with comfort, care, and kindness.

3. **Engagement:** Children need to be truly known and engaged with on a heart level.

4. **Ability to Handle Stimulation:** Children need help effectively regulating the bodily sensations they feel during heightened moments of distress.

5. **Strength Enough to Handle Negative Emotions:** Children need to be free to express the full breadth of their emotions and know deep down that they're accepted and allowed.

6. **Willingness to Repair:** Parents can build healthy attachment with children by building trust through owning their mistakes and rectifying any harm done.[4†]

Conflict is inevitable, even between parents and children. It's not a lack of conflict that indicates a successful relationship with a child; it's actually how we steward those hard moments with kids (especially those coming from a traumatic past) that can make the most positive impact. As Dr. Garry Landreth states, "What's most important may not be what you do, but what you do after what you did."[5]

I clearly remember engaging in silly fights with my sisters through the years. Like any sibling, I'd become angry with them over inconsequential things. Often, genuinely out of my parents' best intentions, they would reprimand my behavior, and I'd face consequences to learn a lesson. However, the underlying emotions

---

† You can find a more extensive description and free materials on Young's website at adamyoungcounseling.com, which I highly recommend.

that had led to my actions in the first place would not be addressed. Therefore, I'd continue to act out or rebel as a result of those unhealed hurts.

What I didn't know how to communicate was that I actually needed someone to be curious about my emotions and memories. I longed for anyone to ask, "Hey, what's going on with you? How's your heart? Why are you acting like this?"

Darin would later explain to me that trauma impacts people in three ways:

> 1. **Fragmentation** occurs when we become overwhelmed by a situation that makes no sense in the moment. When our brain faces a situation that is too difficult/irrational to face all at once, those bits of information become scattered, like puzzle pieces being thrown into the air. These events can't be formed into solid, cohesive, rational memories, especially when we're too young and lack the language abilities to properly process and store the information. Because of the horrors I witnessed as a child in a war zone, my young brain couldn't find a way to rationally process such barbaric events. From that moment forward, fragmentation helped me survive in highly traumatic situations. But that left many gaps in my story. Gaps I needed to fill.

> 2. **Dissociation** is another survival response that occurs when something feels too overwhelming to

face. This is when people go blank trying to recall an event in their past, or when we repress memories from our most painful experiences. Our brain tries to shield us from the pain. By dissociating from my traumatic past, I was able to keep moving forward … until the strategy didn't serve me anymore.

3. Isolation occurs when people have been treated very poorly. They begin to believe that it's easier to care for themselves than to bear bad care from others. At times of pain, I isolated myself from loved ones, trying to convince myself I didn't need anyone and that I was doing okay on my own. As a community-minded man, this never worked out well for me in the long run.

When I was a teenager and young adult, these trauma responses presented themselves in different ways. Often, I wanted to check out from my adopted family and spend as much time as I could away from home. I thought my past was something I should forget about, so I tried my best to do just that. Eventually, something would trigger my past wounds, and I would act out. I believed I wasn't worthy of affection or a true place in my family, so I would try to stop relying on others and find my own way forward.

Just as we all have unique fingerprints and personalities, everyone responds to trauma of any kind differently. Kids are going to be adopted from various cultures. They are going to all have different experiences. While research and some tips from this book are hopefully going to be helpful, nothing will compare to the education you're going to receive in the very real moments you spend with your child. And that's the key. Don't just expect your adopted or fostered child to learn you and your family. Learn your child, too.

Darin kept reiterating to me something that I want to leave you with too: this is a journey. Welcoming a foreign child into your home is a wild adventure. But when you're a family, you're journeying together. Deciding to take it step by step, day by day, together is what really matters most.

This is my book, and I'm offering myself as an example here. My hopes are always that in sharing my story, God will use my experiences to help as many people as possible. So here's a little of what those first steps were like for me, when I finally learned to look back at my trauma so I could move forward and heal.

I had been so accustomed to living with pain, I honestly didn't notice I was hurting until a few years after I came to America. Maybe this was because I had become comfortable living in survival mode since early childhood. Or perhaps it's just my personality to avoid pain if possible. Either way, I had learned at a young age to live with my hurt. It never occurred to me that I needed to heal.

Not until … I got my first job.

Art owned (and still owns) a Chick-fil-A franchise in the Charlotte area. So my first job in high school was serving "Jesus chicken." If you haven't heard Chick-fil-A chicken called this, then you're missing out. Truett Cathy, the food chain's former CEO, upheld Christian principles within the restaurants, and many would claim the chicken is pretty *heavenly*. Yup, Chick-fil-A's fried chicken has appropriately earned the nickname "Jesus chicken." Amen?

Being submerged in a Christian work culture on the Chick-fil-A staff inspired me to read my Bible again. Plus, I spent hours every shift standing in a restaurant where worship music always played in the background. God really began to use His Word to speak to me and give me the courage I needed to grow and heal. On top of that, I started to dwell a little less on my fear and hurt because, when you're in the service industry, your main focus is serving others.

I could barely speak the English language, but people needed their chicken. They didn't care if I had a Liberian accent or if my skin was darker than most. As long as I was putting the right food in the right bag ... they were happy. So my confidence began to build as I helped others and, in response to every "thank you," I repeated the phrase "my pleasure" about a thousand times a day.

Not to brag but (okay, maybe to brag a little) I started my job barely able to speak the English language and ended as one of the best team members on the registers and at the drive through. It was throughout my years on Chick-fil-A's team that I started to settle into the new life God gave me. I also began to effectively communicate with friends and family about what was going on in my life, and I finally exited fight-or-flight mode because I knew I had found a place where I was safe.

After serving at Chick-fil-A, I went on to take a gap year before college to attend the Impact 360 Institute. I shared with you a little bit about this earlier in the book, but during this year, along with my group of institute fellows, I received leadership training from

Chick-fil-A, Inc. I not only learned from Christian leaders from around the country, but I also got to take an incredible mission trip to Brazil. There, everything I had learned as a team member was compounded. I realized that I could not only survive in America, but I now truly began to believe that I could possibly thrive. Even greater, maybe I could become a Christian leader in my generation and bring my story to my new country.

I was given the challenge here to grow, and I stepped right up to answer it.

As I became an adult, I began to distinguish how wide the gap was between who I wanted to be and who I was. Before leaving the house, I always felt like I had to put on a mask and pretend to be optimistic and happy. At some point, I just couldn't fake it anymore.

Amanda was one of the few people who knew the true Jackson TerKeurst. She also saw glimpses of Cammué, my former self. While I didn't know how to reconcile these two versions of myself so they could live in the same place, Amanda could see me as a whole man. She shared with me that the Jackson mask I was wearing might be an attempt at hiding anxiety and depression caused by all the trauma I had gone through. Together, we made an appointment to see my doctor.

After running several tests, the doctor shared that I "definitely [had] anxiety and minor depression that could potentially get worse if left untreated." So I started taking an antidepressant and booked an appointment to see a counselor. Within weeks of taking the medication and meeting with a counselor to process everything I had gone through in the years prior, I began to see a huge difference in my mood.

Finally, I didn't need to rely as heavily on the mask. My past and present started to collide in a beautiful way.

> My past had purpose, and it wasn't to cause me present pain. Everything I had gone through had made me who I am. >>>>>

During this process, I became more intentional about finding a community that knew who I was and loved me exactly as I am. They wanted to see me healthy, and I caught on to their vision and God's plan for my life. My past had purpose, and it wasn't to cause me present pain. Everything I had gone through had made me who I am.

When I started to heal, I began to realize that I could reach out and heal others who had endured trauma too.

Which leads me to where I am today, sitting here writing this book. I'm confronting so many of the memories that I've held on to so I can let them go and allow God to use them to set others free too. We can look at our stories and see how God separates us from our sin and heals the pain that others have inflicted on us. However, He doesn't let us lose the lessons we've learned. Where we once carried a wound, God hands us a weapon and tells us to help others fight their battles too.

The right counsel and advice from the right people will always move us forward.

Take Action

After we do the really hard but incredible work of getting advice on how to heal from our past, we can begin to take action. Here are a few steps that helped me and will hopefully help you move forward into the hope and future God has planned for us all. Keep in mind, these are just to help you start moving in the right direction. I'm not a counselor or expert in these areas; I just unfortunately have a lot of experience from my own healing journey. Be sure you and/or your family continue to lock arms with a faith-based, licensed counselor and healthy community as you find healing.

1. Seek healthy communities based on what you and your family need.

Do not give just anyone full access to your life; your story is sacred. My first recommendation of spaces to begin to build authentic community will always be church and Bible studies/groups with fellow believers because prayer is powerful and vulnerability has chain-breaking power. Really close friends and family also fall into this category. When you can open up about the pain of your past, it starts to lose its power. We need people we can openly share with who can be trusted with our stories and will hold the weight of it all as we collectively place our past in the hands of God.

2. Seek mentorship, counseling, and accountability.

Moving forward doesn't mean forgetting and moving on. It's the remembering of our past and mistakes that reminds us where to put our feet as we start taking steps. When we're really healing from trauma, we're a little like a baby learning to walk. Mentors and friends who will hold us accountable are vital in helping us move in the right direction. Our faith may have wobbly legs for a time, and these people are the crew that will carry us forward.

3. Cultivate a culture within your home of open conversation.

When we hear the word "culture," we tend to think of people, ethnic groups, or nationalities. However, our businesses, churches, and even homes have a culture. Culture really means the customs of any place, space, or people. Any child who has experienced losing their family really needs parents or caregivers who will be incredibly intentional about creating a home and family culture where conversation is open. If they really want their child to heal, they need to seek to understand their child's story without correction or judgment, with a listening ear and an open heart. The child needs to feel like they can share as little or as much as they feel comfortable, whenever they are ready. As trust builds, they will open up more.

While our physical needs were finally met and we were overflowing spiritually, the next greatest thing my brother and I needed was for someone to take the time to learn our stories. We longed for our personalities and culture to be celebrated. This was something my family did really well. My parents read books, went to conferences about this, and developed a support system with other moms who had also adopted kids from Liberia so we could all share best practices and regularly provide opportunities to keep us culturally connected. Our family made space for our memories to be heard, joys to be laughed at, and sorrow to be cried over with us. Open conversation allowed us to wade into the waters of our past over time.

We had a weekly family tradition we called "Monday night dinners," where all of us opened up about our lives past and present. I very much participated in these special weekly family conversations. Emotions were expressed. Hurts were shared. Joys were celebrated. Sorrows were comforted. And it was very common for my brother and me to cook African food in our home—and all of us have many funny stories about this. Not only that, but my parents made sure to get counselors involved to help me navigate my trauma.

There is no burying our past. What's done is done. So there is only digging it up, holding out the mess to God, and asking Him to sift it like dirt. We ask Him to show us the gold and treasures He hid in the sand and then beg Him to wash away the muck and stains on our own hands. Through taking advice and acting on it, we're left with healed scars and not open wounds. And that is how we go forward, healed and whole.

That's enough advice. Now, back to my story …

Section 8

THE PAST MEETS THE PRESENT

Simba: I know what I have to do, but going back means I'll have to face my past. I've been running from it for so long.

[Rafiki hits Simba on the head with his stick]

Simba: Ow! Jeez! What was that for?

Rafiki: It doesn't matter. It's in the past.

Simba: Yeah, but it still hurts.

Rafiki: Oh yes, the past can hurt. But the way I see it, you can either run from it or learn from it.

Disney's *The Lion King*

It's quiet on the twenty-third floor of our uptown apartment building tonight. Though it's been almost two decades since I lived in a war zone, I still find myself noting every noise. A car backfiring. A muffled conversation outside the apartment next door. A police car siren wailing off in the distance. I never know what I'm specifically listening for anymore, but I still always and forever will want to keep a pulse on the world around me. As I learned to do as a kid, I block out all my other senses and intently listen. Anything? Not really. Surprisingly, only the hum of Charlotte traffic seems to be keeping me company tonight.

Amanda has already gone to bed because she is the early bird. I'm the night owl, alone with my thoughts. Maybe I need a little company tonight. In addition to constantly keeping tabs on my surroundings, I also rely on other old habits to fill the silence. When I was a kid in Liberia, we used to listen to the BBC on the radio. So as an adult, I flip to the news on TV when the house becomes too quiet. *Where is that remote?* Click.

The dark screen lights up, not with the expected picture of a news anchor reciting the latest story from a desk, but with foreign faces of people in panic and distress. The muffled city background noise is replaced with the familiar sounds of people screaming as bombs explode. Children lie bloody on the streets or in body bags. Families are ripped tragically from their homes. The headlines scrolling along the bottom of the screen read that Russia is at war with Ukraine. "This is only the beginning," a reporter's voice solemnly concludes.

"Escape! Run for your lives!" I want to shout at the TV and set free all the Ukrainian victims. But I know they can't hear me. I know they can't escape. I know it all too well.

My own breath starts to quicken. My heart is racing. I am no longer in my living room on the twenty-third floor of an uptown apartment with my loving wife sleeping peacefully in the safety of the next room. Instead, with brush underfoot and bombs exploding in the distance, huts on fire and women screaming, I too am back in a war zone and running for my life in Liberia.

Blink. Breathe. Come back to reality. This isn't happening to me; it's happening on a screen. It's someone else's real life across the ocean. It's not me anymore in Liberia, but another little boy running for his life in Ukraine.

I take a moment to come back to the present, easing away from the horrors of the flashback. As my world rights itself, my heart shatters for the innocent lives, especially the children, affected by yet another barbaric war.

To the Child Survivors of a Present-Day War

As the TV light casts shadows across my apartment, I pace my living room floor wishing I could talk to these victims. I start to think about what I would say if I could have a raw, real conversation with the children who survive war. I'd squat down to their level and place my hands gently but firmly on their shoulders. I'd look them in the eye and, through silent tears and a half smile, I'd say something like:

> Listen, you're not alone. I hate war. It scares me too and still makes me feel unsettled. War took away my family, my childhood, my peace and comfort, and replaced that with anxiety and depression, stress, and feelings of abandonment and loneliness.
>
> War robs us because it steals our innocence. We shouldn't have to know what it's like to look into the eyes of dead people. We should have never witnessed murder or heard the screams of those being terrorized. No child should be robbed of

safety, family, innocence, love, and affection. I'm so unbelievably sorry you have gone through this and that you now know what it takes to survive a war.

But you did survive! And that's not by chance.

There is no doubt about it—going through war, being torn from your family, and surviving such extreme trauma will have long-lasting effects on your psyche. A lot of times it won't seem fair. You'll long for justice and you'll have no power to make everything all right.

Without facing those demons head on, you will probably harbor a lot of resentment, hurt, and anger. But take the Bible's advice and "be strong and courageous" (Josh. 1:6). Seek a healthy community. Set goals and put yourself in positions where you can learn, grow, and be poured into in a positive way. Serve others so you don't become selfish and self-preserving. Heal from your trauma. Seek God. He created you, and He has a plan to use what you have been through.

It's going to be hard but good as you do the internal work to look back, heal from your past, and move forward to pursue God's plan for your life. With God's help and support from your community, you can do anything! I believe in you.

We are survivors. We survived these horrors so we can help others come alive in Jesus and be set free. So, rest. Heal. And remember. Because the only way forward is back.

To the Parents Who Adopt Them

My mind's eye looks up from the imaginary child who was before me to see the parents who will adopt them. I rise to my full height as my previous half smile begins to spread full across my face. In a "thank you," I hug them and settle into saying:

You are in for a treat! And a challenge. I think this will be one of the most rewarding experiences of your life because you're parenting one of the strongest kids out there, a true survivor.

Your child may not have answers right away, but ask them questions about their experience. Be curious about their life before the war. Ask for details about what they went through, and allow them to celebrate the positive and happy memories they still hold from their home country.

Stay genuinely and courageously curious. Be patient and let them know you're there for them to talk through those things when they're ready. Make them feel heard when they do speak.

As you learn from your child, also seek outside sources like books and support groups to grow in your understanding of the cultural and socioeconomic differences your child is facing. Always stand on the love of Jesus and point out similarities that unify you. Perhaps you both have the same favorite color, love a particular movie, like the same candy, laugh at a particular joke, etc.

As children, they may not yet realize they need help, but walk with your child through counseling and surround them and your family with a healthy community. Help them heal and never rush them through the process. This is going to take time, but now you have forever to be a family. And family is everything.

Learn to parent from your heavenly Father. As He adopted us, you too are bringing in one of His children into your home. You are giving them a space where they are safe, where they belong, and where they can rediscover their identity as they rest and restore.

On their behalf and mine, thank you. Thank you. Thank you.

I wipe a silent tear, turn off the TV, and crawl into bed next to Amanda. Despite my positive imaginary speeches to Child Survivor and Adoptive Parents, a horrible feeling remains in my gut. I have to tell Amanda about how intense that flashback was. After all, we are all always healing.

On Flashbacks ...

Not all flashbacks are as rough as this one. While I recall a lot of war, grief, death, and poverty, I actually tend to look back more at my time in Liberia with a sense of rosy retrospection. I think about my childhood and even moments in the orphanage with fondness. With longing, I recall the food, music, emphasis on community, and time with my Liberian loved ones.

When I have a good flashback, I reach for rice and cook African food full of flavor and spice. I turn up the Afrobeats and start singing and dancing along to the music. I remember what it's like to be part of a village and tribe, and I strike up conversations with random people I pass in the city. They look at me funny but, at that moment, I'm proudly Liberian and don't care.

Now, I am also proudly American. I love this country's strong sense of patriotism, the safety of living here in the land of the free, the abundance of opportunities, and the ability for even an African immigrant like me to chase their dreams. There's so much good here. Over the years, I also had a rosy outlook on integrating into the culture and didn't realize that I had fully "Americanized" until I was an adult.

I was in my thirties, standing in front of a TV watching coverage of the war in Ukraine, when I took off my rose-colored glasses about this place. Suddenly, I became aware that I'd bought into the American lie that I need to be independent. It's like everyone hits eighteen in this country and they are expected to be on their own, surviving away from their family. Thriving on your own and viewing everyone else climbing the ladder toward your American dream as competition … as if that's something to take pride in. America is a place where we all pretend we don't need anyone. We are known for "picking ourselves up by the bootstraps" and "moving forward" without ever daring to ask for help (much less expecting it to come our way). Where once I considered myself a part of a village, I had to look at my adult life and admit that I had bought into the American lie that relying on a group of people meant I was weak.

The reality: I need other people. I still want to belong to a village. We all do. Now I have reliable handles for how to deal with the trauma of my past, but my wife, our friends, community, and church are the people who remind me to hold on to them when I start to let go.

There are a lot of things I like about America. But I'm going to have to stand by the Liberian thought that, when the rose-colored glasses come off, we all need people to help us see.

Amanda is that person for me. She's my eyes when I don't want to look at the past because it hurts too much.

It took me a minute to talk about being triggered by the war on TV. The truth is, I was afraid. No part of me was eager to go back and relive the war that I had barely survived the first time. But I've learned that if I keep my struggles a secret, they seem to grow in the dark. Talking about them turns the light on, and there the nightmares and flashbacks begin to shrink.

So I let go of my defenses, and I told Amanda everything. How I had watched the war on the news. How I had been absolutely wrecked by seeing all the children who were displaced. How I could not stop thinking about the image of a child left alone on a bomb-torn street, crying for his parents as dead bodies had been left all around him. How that image was now seared into my brain. How in that child, I saw me.

"Don't turn on any channels with the news. I can't take it anymore," I pleaded to her. And she listened. Not just heard me. She truly listened, like she always does. The news didn't come back on TV.

On the Reality of the American Dream ...

Something I can't seem to turn off in this season is how much I sometimes feel like a failure in the workplace. Growing up, I couldn't wait to chase the American dream, and now I realize it's all a fantasy. It's a dangling carrot you never catch. God. Jesus. Love. Those are the only true things in life.

Here's why I struggle in the workspace. In Liberia, people don't have one specific job or career type they necessarily choose and stick with for life. Your trade is ever changing depending on what your family specializes in or what your community needs at the time. Life is lived on a day-to-day basis.

Here in America, everything is about having a plan and creating more, more, more wealth. I remember being asked constantly as a teenager here, "What are you going to do when you grow up? What do you want to be?" *Was I really supposed to know the answer to that question as a teenager? Are my worth and identity based solely on my work accomplishments? Will I ever do or be enough in this country where money is sometimes worshipped more than God?*

Though my biological dad had inspired me to study business, choosing a permanent career path never really felt natural to me because of my upbringing. I've always had what Americans would call an "entrepreneurial mindset." I want to make things happen. I want to see an idea grow, help others, and build up a community.

As a result, it's been so hard over the years to remain in a stagnant job while my life seems to constantly be shifting. I've felt locked down when I should be unlocking doors and opportunities for my family.

I've never felt free in an American career because I can't make my own choices or spark true change. I feel like another machine producing a product, not a person living out my true passion. This can feel like torture sometimes for someone whose formative years were spent cultivating a tribal mindset (not individual dreams but collective goals) and living on African time (never even hearing of a nine to five).

I talk to Amanda about this struggle a lot. She goes along with my wild ideas (like writing a book). And she helps me make decisions when I'm paralyzed by fear.

You see, if there's one right choice I've ever made, it was choosing Amanda to be my wife. She remains my go-to person. My ride-or-die. I can tell her anything, and I know she will love me anyway. When I'm weak (which is more often than I want to admit), she helps me be strong. And sometimes I get the honor of being that person for her too.

While I struggle mentally and with my occupation, Amanda has physically walked through hell and come out on the other side. I wouldn't change holding her hand through that for anything.

On Growing a Family ...

My wife is my village now. We're trying to add onto our little tribe by two tiny feet. Or four. Or six! But adding at least one baby has been hard enough. After a year of trying to conceive, we've yet to see God answer our prayer for a baby.

Amanda has gone to the doctor to determine what might be going on. *Where is our baby? Why isn't she or he here yet? What did the doctor say?* The moment she walks in the door with tears streaming down her face, her answer falls like rocks into my gut.

"We won't be able to have kids naturally." She verbally answers my thoughts, and I'm speechless.

In the two-second break before she explains, my brain jumps to a thousand conclusions that rattle off like a machine gun. *It's because I was sick for so long in the orphanage and was never treated until I came to the States. Or what if it's because of the witch that cursed my family with the inability to have kids? What if those witches have somehow found out about Amanda and me, and they have taken it a step further and done some crazy voodoo on us from Liberia? What if God is punishing me for something I did wrong? What if ...*

"My fallopian tubes are blocked," Amanda explains. "The doctors could not find a cause relating to my medical history. Apparently there are several products that women use that carry a ton of junk in them. This can be one of the side effects."

Of course, her explanation is much more rational than my thought process, but still ... while I'm a little glad there's nothing horrifically wrong with either one of us, the perfect picture I had of my future family starts to crack. I feel helpless and useless. I'm devastated. And, surprisingly, I'm mostly mad.

When my family was taken away from me as a boy in Liberia … when I witnessed death and rape … when I was starving and suffering … when my adoptive family fell apart … I don't really remember being mad at God. Mad at other people? Sure. But not at God.

Well, there's a first time for everything. And today, for the first time, I'm very mad at God.

We sit down on the couch and keep crying. Amanda keeps apologizing, and I tell her this isn't her fault. I know this doesn't make anything better, but I don't know much else to say at this moment. It's not her fault. It's not mine either. Yet I'm sorry too. I'm sorry God won't let us have a baby.

Why would God take away the chance for two people who have had their families ripped apart to create one of their own? This is NOT the rosy picture of how growing our family looked in my mind. Watching my wife cry like this was never part of the plan. God, I'm mad.

I hold Amanda, trying to be strong and optimistic for her. But I'm still fuming, and I don't really feel like I have anyone to talk to about it. I can't put my finger on the other emotion I'm feeling, but the closest I can get is embarrassed.

Desperately, we need and want support. A village of our own. Yet we don't want anyone to know what we're going through. *Does God not think we're capable of carrying and creating a family? Is this how it goes for us? Do we never get to restore and take back what the enemy has stolen?*

Here's the issue again with the pressure here in American culture to be so independent and self-sufficient. If we don't come to God, confess our weaknesses, and share with others our struggles, we spend our days making choices we think will heal our own hurt.

That is exactly what I was doing. In an attempt to hide or numb my anger, I was actually making my life revolve around redirecting it. I was hard on myself and short with Amanda. I was bitter toward God. All my actions were actually just reactions to my suppressed emotions, and the world around me suffered for it.

I needed someone to help me set aside the rose-colored glasses and the picture-perfect vision of our future family. I needed someone to look me in the eye and show me the harsh reality of my present situation while pointing me toward the hope of what my future could be.

I needed a trusted member of my village, as we all do when life is hard. Because tribes help us thrive. Amanda had always been my person, but now she was fighting her own pain. I needed to talk to someone else.

So I finally opened up to a friend.

> **I needed a trusted member of my village, as we all do when life is hard. Because tribes help us thrive.**

"Why do all these terrible things in life keep happening to me?" I long for any answer my friend will give me. Anything that can ground my soul in faith again.

"You have lived through hell. You and your family were being hunted like animals, and God got you through that situation. He brought you where you're at today," my friend reminds me. "Amanda is a good girl. She loves you more than anything, and I have seen it since I first introduced the both of y'all to each other in college. Keep trusting in God and do everything in your power to be there for her. Imagine how terrible you are feeling right now. She's feeling twice as hurt compared to you. You need to be strong and stay faithful to Him."

Honestly, that reality check hurts, but I need it. I look at my friend and encourage him to keep talking. Which he does.

"The Devil is trying his hardest to destroy you, but God has called you to be something greater than this. Trust His timing, seek Him, and seek community that will support you and Amanda throughout this process. Be vulnerable and open about what you are experiencing rather than being angry. You're losing the best of you, chasing substances to numb the pain, walking away from Amanda, and keeping your head down.

"The truth is, bro, there are millions of people around the world experiencing infertility. The sad thing is that most of these people are ashamed and afraid to talk about that part of their journey openly. But guidance is vital if you want to succeed in this season.

"Remember that God has chosen you and given you this journey for a reason. You have to expose the Devil. The only way to do that is for you and Amanda to seek help from others on the days that you are feeling low. Pray without ceasing. Most importantly, ditch your pride. Be brave and share your journey on the platform that God has given you. Only then can you help others who are experiencing similar struggles. As you and Amanda find strength, others can too.

"Your story is about more than just you."

Sometimes the past and present collide, and it hurts too much to want to remember or face it. We need someone to hit us over the head with reality and remind us that our God isn't confined to the box of our situation.

So I took my friend's advice. Amanda and I decided to open up to God and others, surround ourselves with a supportive village, and think outside the box. We even shared on social media to allow anyone out there to help pray for us and possibly find some inspiration in their own journey. No, we couldn't conceive on our own, but we truly felt like God was calling us to have our own children. We couldn't give up.

Ultimately, Amanda and I settled on pursuing in vitro fertilization (the fertility process of combining a woman's eggs and man's sperm in a lab and then transferring the fertilized embryo into a woman's body at the ideal time, commonly abbreviated as IVF). We didn't know it then, but we'd continue on this IVF journey for six and a half years. That's a lot of time to doubt and ask questions like

"Are we sure we're still doing this?" "Should we pray about it again?" "Is there another way?"

As I was an adopted kid, we definitely considered adoption as an option. Amanda had thrown the idea out there to try both. We could adopt as we continued trying with IVF and build our family both ways. Surrogacy also came up, but it was too expensive, and ultimately, we weren't sure how we felt about it. We barely had enough money in our account to pay our bills from all the failed IVF transfers over the years. All options were risky and rough. Not to mention physically, emotionally, and spiritually exhausting—especially for Amanda, whose body was put through painful challenges again and again.

Interestingly, what I discovered in all these discussions was that my past and present led to a deep desire to first have children who were my own flesh and blood. Something about the way I was ripped away from my own parents and never feeling like I fully belonged to my adopted family made me want to have kids who couldn't be taken from me and who would never doubt their identity as our children.

As a first-generation Liberian immigrant to America, I also wanted to see my own bloodline start a legacy here for future generations. America, the land of opportunity! The adoption conversation remained open, but we decided to focus on doing everything we could to create our own biological family.

However, our IVF journey was long and hard. We spent a fortune, and Amanda had to undergo surgery and several IVF treatments. There is no way on the face of the planet we could have gone through all that we did if it weren't for our village constantly reminding us of what God has done for us before and what He wants to do for us again.

Funny how when we confess our weakness in community, God sends us a village to make us strong. See, weakness and strength are not mutually exclusive. As believers we can mourn for the past, hurt in the present, and hope for the future all at the same time. Because, though something may seem bad, there is always a good God behind it all. If it's not good, my experiences tell me that He's not finished with it yet.

That is why things can seem like they're not working out at all as we look at our lives, and yet we can still trust the God of impossible to make a miracle possible. And that is exactly what Amanda and I decided to do through it all—trust and believe.

> **Weakness and strength are not mutually exclusive. As believers we can mourn for the past, hurt in the present, and hope for the future all at the same time.** »»»

Ultimately, my friend was right. This story has always been about more than just me. Maybe you too need to learn from your past, face the reality of the present, and believe in God for the good to come.

That's why I titled the book *The Only Way Forward Is Back*. When we look back at what God has brought us through, then we can move forward.

If we're brave enough to believe in Him, things will start to turn around—maybe not exactly how we want, but ultimately for our good and God's glory. And that's what's most important, because life isn't about us. It's about Him.

My story is for you. Your story is for someone else.

When we dare to believe, surrender, trust, and share, only then can God's story be truly told.

Take the Shot

It's Saturday morning, and we're taking the day a little slow. It's the weekend, after all. Amanda is a nurse, so she's been handling our IVF journey over the past few years like a champ. In the two months before an embryo transfer, I watch her attend multiple doctor appointments at seven in the morning before working long shifts as a nurse. I also watch helplessly as she takes hormone pills, gives herself shots, and does everything she possibly can to prepare her body to carry a baby. *Our baby.*

A lot of times I feel helpless. There's nothing I can do beyond supporting my wife and praying my heart out. Also, I hate needles. Which is why I'm confused right now as Amanda is preparing her morning shot and medication. *Why is she looking at me like it's my turn?* I can't take the shot for her (though I do often wish I could shoulder some of the physical struggle), so that could only mean one thing. My hands start to sweat.

"I want you to give me my shot this morning," she says with a smirk.

"No way! I have to stick you with that long needle? You do not want me to do that. I can't do it."

She laughs at me and unfortunately doesn't give me another option. "You have to do at least one shot in the process." *Fine. Dads can do hard things, and I'm going to be a dad!*

I am a brave, strong dad-to-be, but I am not fine. I'm freaking out.

Carefully, in the meticulous way that nurses do, she lays out all the supplies she's prepared—the injection medication, alcohol wipe, and Band-Aid. Handing me the long needle and syringe, she lies down on her side of our bed. She points out to me exactly the spot to inject the needle. Amanda has made this dummy proof, and I'm still afraid I'm going to hit the wrong spot! Hands shaking, again I declare, "Amanda, I cannot do this. No way!"

She gives me an eye that says something between "Get it together" and "I believe in you."

So I comically try to give my wife a shot in her butt. I get close with the needle but, at the last second, I pull back. This happens at least three times. Like children at a sleepover who have stayed up too late, we're cracking up. Every time I try and pull away, the scene gets sillier.

"Just stick the needle in!" She laughs at me.

I take a deep breath and really go for it this time. The tip of the needle is in! Instead of the shot going into her, I feel like nerves are shooting up my arm. In reaction, I pull the needle back out. She's belly laughing at this point and all I can think about is how I just stabbed my wife for absolutely nothing. Amanda could have done this in two seconds, but it's taking me an eternity.

We calm down and reset, and I commit. After the embarrassment I just caused myself, I have to get this one right. My future children are counting on me.

Mentally, I count to three and stick the needle all the way in. Okay there. The needle is in her butt. I freeze.

"Now push the medicine in," Amanda talks to me in the kind, slow, calm voice mothers use for their children when they're teaching them to do something new. Great, she's already got the mom voice down pat, and I can't even give my wife a shot.

On command, I push the medicine through the syringe and pull the needle back out. The nerves that were threatening to rattle my arm off finally release, and I exhale into another bout of laughter. We're cracking up next to each other on the bed. Rolling over I shout, "I will NEVER do that again!"

Let my future children know, their mom is the bravest, most resilient woman alive. I can't put a shot in her butt, but she can, for years, sacrifice her body in the hopes that we can one day have a child of our own. We still believe. We are the TerKeurst Tribe-to-be.

(If we're pregnant after this round, I'm for sure taking the credit.)

On Fighting for Family

Our past and present always collide. With every year that goes by, we are not actually different people. We've just faced different circumstances that change us. Yet, no matter who we are, we are all triggered by memories, seek identity in a family-like unit, desire to be loved, and become a summation of how we interpret all our experiences.

We are who we were then and now. Yes, God separates our sin from us, but He purposefully does not let us lose the lessons we've learned. He turns our wounds into weapons so we can fight back.

For me,
my past and present collide at this thought:
If I don't want the fight to take my family out,
as a man, I need to fight for my family.

The hardest part of the IVF journey isn't necessarily the physical struggle. I know you're thinking, "Of course he would say that. He's a dude!" And you're right. It wasn't my body that had to go through the meds and shots and surgery. However, Amanda and I would both agree that the worst part is the extreme emotional roller coaster. When you think that maybe this time, it might be it! This could be the Christmas we get to put another stocking on the mantel. This could be the year we set up a nursery. This could be our turn to make the pregnancy announcement. But the test reads negative … again. Our hopes get thrown up and down like a yo-yo, reaching high and low extremes.

To fight well for the family we felt God was calling us to build, we had to learn to not be yanked around on the emotional roller coaster. Emotions are valid. God gave them to us, and He has them Himself.

- God gets angry. (Deut. 9:22; Ps. 7:11)
- God has compassion. (Judg. 2:18; Ps. 135:14)
- God loves. (John 3:16; 1 John 4:8)

- God hates. (Ps. 5:5; Prov. 6:16)
- God is jealous. (Ex. 20:5; Josh. 24:19)
- God is joyous. (Isa. 62:5; Zeph. 3:17)

But there's one main difference when it comes to God's emotions versus ours. God always has pure, sinless motivations with the big picture in mind. We have selfish motivations and can only see the very moment in front of us.

While we can't escape or ignore our feelings, we can bring the way we feel to the God who fully understands our highest highs and lowest lows. We can ask that He will give us strength to keep fighting when our soul sits at the bottom. And we can create our own village by sharing our pain and hopes with others we trust.

If you're fighting for your family, proactively note this: It's okay to be hurt and feel hopeless at times. It's also okay to get your hopes up and stay optimistic. Fight for your family by being vulnerable about those emotions. Fight for your family by caring for your marriage relationship. Fight for your family by doing what you can to care for yourself emotionally, physically, and spiritually. Be active, eat well, and seek wise counsel. Most of all, trust that God will bring you answers as He has planned. He may, as He usually does, move in a way you least expect.

If you feel knocked down because your family situation has taken a few unexpected turns, remember that you're not knocked out. You have a God who was fighting for you in the past. He's fighting for you and your family now. So stand firm on the strong foundation of God and keep fighting!

Section 9

WHERE ARE THEY NOW?

Over the past twenty-three seasons, Oprah has met hundreds of families and heard many heartwarming stories, but she says this is one of her all-time favorites.... In the two years since Oprah first heard their story, eight more families in the community opened their homes to eleven more children—a total of forty-four children, with more on the way!

Oprah's OWN, "Love Knows No Color"

When a boys' choir made the journey from their home country, Liberia, to a North Carolina church to raise money, they had no idea how their lives were about to change. When one of the churchgoers, Lysa TerKeurst, learned that twelve of the boys from the choir became homeless when their orphanage was destroyed in Liberia's brutal civil war, she decided to adopt two of them, Jackson and Mark. Families in Lysa's community were inspired to join in, and since then, more than forty children from the same orphanage have been adopted, including all twelve choirboys. How have Jackson and Mark, now in their twenties, adjusted to life with the TerKeursts? It's the update Oprah says she's been waiting to hear!

Oprah's OWN, "Where Are They Now?" season 2, episode 215

As a boy, I didn't have access to a TV. The only familiarity I had with talking, moving technology boxes were movies that played in fancy theaters in America. The only characters I really knew of were the ones that were famous in West Africa—Commando, Chuck Norris, and Rambo. That was it.

When our story surfaced, the nation was inspired by Lysa's willingness to welcome Mark and me into the family. So much attention was drawn to our adoption—along with the forty-four other Liberian orphans who ended up making their way into the safety of American families as a result—that Oprah noticed. She was so moved that she wanted to interview our family. This was a HUGE deal, but I had very little clue how special this opportunity really was.

After our appearance on *Oprah*, we had a few things written about us. Years later, they did a follow-up story on the Oprah Winfrey Network (OWN) as part of a segment called "Where Are They Now?"

Step back with me to this pivotal moment when I was still in college and we were all on set at the show. Then we'll move forward to answer some important questions.

Oprah Winfrey heard about our adoption story and wanted to interview us. The minute my mom told us about this opportunity, I thought, *Wow! Who's Oprah Winfrey?*

The only Black actress I'm really aware of is Whoopi Goldberg from the *Sister Act* movies I watched with the choir boys years ago.

So I ask my brother Mark to clue me in on who we're talking about here.

Mark quickly reminds me that Oprah was the lady we watched the other day on the living room TV. "Remember? She was giving away free cars!"

Ohhhhh, yeah. "What if she gifted us Range Rovers as our first American cars?" I dream in response.

Like best friends, we joke back and forth about all sorts of outlandish things we could receive from Oprah. Together, we drop dead laughing. It all feels like a joke because the opportunity to be on TV with one of the greatest hostesses in the nation doesn't seem real for boys like us.

"The camera will be here any minute. Boys, are you ready?" Mom calls through the house.

"Yup," we respond back. Of course we're ready. Our outfits have been laid out for days because we're so excited to be on television.

"Girls," Lysa's voice echoes again from downstairs. "Are you almost ready?"

All three of my sisters respond with some version of "Yes, almost." They'd better hurry up because the camera crew just arrived at the house.

Groups of people with big black bags of equipment begin to take over our living spaces. All of a sudden, it really sinks in that this isn't a joke. Lights and cameras are going up everywhere confirming the reality that we're about to be on TV. *Gah, now I'm really nervous!*

"Mark, wanna go play 'Horse' on the basketball court until these people are done?" This isn't a question. I'm pleading for an escape.

"Yes, please, bro." He wants to get out of here as much as I do.

We start heading outside and ease into a quick game. It feels normal for a moment, and our nerves settle to the familiar rhythm of the dribble of the ball until Mark asks in disbelief, "Are all these people with these cameras really here for us?"

I shrug. "I guess so." I try to be nonchalant, but my palms are sweating as I go up for a shot.

"Boys, we need you. The producer called for us," Mom yells across the yard.

Upon entering the house, we walk straight into a crew-led debrief on the questions Oprah will be asking us and other details we need to know for being on camera. Then, Mom tells me something that makes me want to throw up and dance at the same time. "Oprah would like to interview you, Jackson. They want to interview Mark too, but they're especially interested in hearing about your recent trip back to Liberia."

"Shut up! Me? Why me?" I ask. "I can't do this."

"Sure, you can. You are one of the smartest, most articulate, and driven boys I know. And, of course, you're handsome."

She's trying to butter me up so I'll feel a little better about this, I just know it. I soak up all the encouragement anyway.

"You have such an incredible story, son, and I think you should tell it to the world."

Her last line fires me up. My nerves seem dull now compared to how excited I am to shine a light on all God has done in my life. I want the world to see. It's showtime, baby.

Lights. Camera. Action.

During the actual interview, my mom is first spotlighted. Sitting in our living room, she shares a recap of our backstory, educational struggles, and update on our lives. At that time, I'm still studying at Union University and Mark is coaching soccer.

The scene then cuts to my interview. I share about my trip back to Africa where I got to serve as a missionary. We discuss all the emotion I experienced returning to my homeland.

"Liberia is the country that shaped me.... I'm going to go back always," I conclude after a stream of photos from my trip comes to an end.

Mark shows off his piano and soccer skills in a few clips and talks about being protective of our sisters. You can pop over to Oprah.com and watch all three minutes of it. It's wholesome and sweet.

However, if I were a director and could recreate a special for you today, I would play out the following scenes as a response to the statement my mom made to me a decade ago before that Oprah Winfrey Network interview:

"You have such an incredible story, son," she said. "I think you should tell it to the world."

For me, the *Tell It to the World* Jackson TerKeurst Special would look something like this ...

Scene I: Where Are They Now? A Post-Civil War Special

Time fast-forwards. I'm a young man now. Lights up on me sitting on my bed after a long day of work.

My phone rings, and I see that it's my brother Jerry calling from Liberia. I answer quickly.

"Hello, Cammué. I'm here with someone who wants to speak with you."

My heart feels like it's about to beat out of my chest. *Who could it be? Who did they find?*

"Hello ... hello ... Cammué?" I recognize the voice as if it were my own. Immediately, I jump out of my seat with as much excitement as I would if someone had told me I had won the lottery. Maybe I just had.

"Nae Keyneh*?" *O'ma?*

"Yes, my son!" The woman replies sweetly in my native language as my brother interprets. Immediately, the child in me recognizes my mother's voice, her laugh. I latch onto her words as if they are pearls up for grabs because it's been so long since I've heard her voice. This moment is a treasure. My mom is alive!

All at once, I feel like I am home. Yet I'm so far away. I would give anything to see her face, give her the world's biggest, longest hug, and catch up after all these years. I'm laughing with tears in my eyes as my long-tended spark of hope catches full flame. No longer do I have to worry if my mom is alive. She no longer has to worry if her oldest son made it through the war. We are alight. We are alive!

Time fast-forwards a few weeks. Lights come up on my brother,
Jerry, still searching other parts of the country after finding my
mom. He's like a marine sent out on a rescue mission in the
middle of the night, determined to find our father. Finally, he
locates him in the neighboring town of Gbarnga ...

There he is, our dad. Alive! Jerry can't believe it. Dad can't believe
it. Dad then tells his war story like it's his darkest secret, one he's
relieved to finally uncover. It goes something like this:

When Dad was taken away by rebels, he was one of the few who
got to choose to "make it to heaven or hell." He chose hell.

As a result, he was taken away and imprisoned, starved, beaten,
and basically left for dead on the floor with other men who suffered
his same torture. They awaited judgment from the rebel leader, and
Dad spent what he believed were his last moments thinking of his
family.

The leader divided the group into two. Those on the left would
be beheaded, and those on the right would be set free. When my
dad's name was called, something miraculous happened. A soldier
he'd met years back remembered my father. When he and his family
were going through hardship, my father had used what little he'd had
to help that man's family. The soldier recalled my dad's name and
was so moved by his former act of kindness that he spoke up for him.

"Henson Gweh, is that you?" the man asked my dad.

As Dad confirmed his identity, the man pleaded with his commander in charge to save Dad's life, vouching that my father was a

good man. By the grace of God, the commander granted the man's wish because he was a trusted soldier.

The soldier then took Dad in his army truck to the nearby village and told him where he could see some of the relatives he had spotted a while back during his patrol. In Liberia, word travels fast, and the story reached my extended family, so they sent my brother Jerry to find out if it was true. And it was! Dad was alive!

The soldier and Jerry corresponded, and they made a plan to secretly drop my dad off in a location where they could reconnect in the town of Gbarnga. When they reunited in the city, Jerry knew Dad had to remain in hiding for his own safety, so he took Dad to a village tucked deep in the jungle where the rest of my family had been hiding. When it was safe, Jerry and Dad tried to locate me. They went from orphanages to refugee camps and churches searching for me, finding nothing.

Finally, they made it to Monrovia, the town that hosted my orphanage, Monrovia Home. "Your boy has traveled overseas," Daniel, a "big brother" from the same tribe as me who was still living there, told them. They were sad to not see me but relieved to learn that I was safe.

Commercial break.

This is the part of the story where the commercial or ad pops up and you're mad about it. I know what you're thinking … *Jackson's parents survived! WHAT! Does this story ever get a happy ending?*

Calm down, I'm about to tell you.

Most of my family couldn't afford a phone, so to contact me abroad, they did what people have been doing for centuries. They wrote and mailed me a letter—old-school style. After borrowing a pen and piece of paper from Daniel, my father wrote one of these "snail mail" letters to let me know that most of the family made it out of the war alive, including my mother.

I wanted so badly to believe that the letter was real, but somewhere deep down I doubted. It all felt too good to be true. Someone could be pulling my leg, like they tend to do in Liberia, pretending to be a loved one just to get money from me. Or worse, what if this was some twisted fairy tale I had tumbled into that may not end in happily ever after?

My questions made me want to bring the whole situation up to Art and Lysa, but with all the divorce drama surfacing on the internet about our American family, their world was turning upside down. And so was mine. I didn't want to add any stress to the TerKeurst family, so I decided I needed to see my birth parents first. My biological parents being alive might be a hard pill for Art and Lysa to swallow.

On top of the family drama, Amanda and I were still struggling with infertility. I could tell I was forgetting, just like I had in college, what it was like to have community and family. Again, I needed my village, to feel the African dirt between my toes. I desperately wanted—NEEDED—to see my Liberian parents!

I reached back out to Jerry to tell him that I was planning to travel back home to Liberia to see my birth family. I was going to rent an apartment where everyone could stay.

Jerry anxiously ran and told just a few of my biological family members that I was coming, while I let my adopted family know about my trip. With the little money I had saved for the trip, I loaded three bags filled with clothes, shoes, hygiene products, and essential items. I called up the airline and booked my flight, made sure all my shots and passport were up to date, and even drove up to DC to get my Liberian visa.

The only thing I forgot was trip insurance.

Scene change. I'm 30,000 feet up in the air on a flight from Brussels to Roberts International Airport in Liberia. It's a similar travel scene to my college trip except now it's 2021 and I'm in my early 30s. My headphones are blasting Afrobeats, and I'm excitedly looking out the airplane window.

I have been keeping up with my family while traveling, and what's getting me through on this leg of the trip is remembering when my little brother Emmanuel video chatted with me on WhatsApp with my mom from the apartment. I can't stop picturing her smile and hearing her laugh. In just a few moments, I'll get to see her in person.

The lights go darker on the set as the airplane lands. I exit with my luggage into the terminal.

It's dark when I land in Liberia. I'm a weird mix of exhausted and excited as I'm shuffled through the noisy, chaotic terminal. I stand in a single-file line as an employee collects my passport with a fifty-dollar fee. Next, they send me to a team member who administers a Covid test. I now sit and wait for my result. Negative. Thank God.

Another employee asks for a document from America that states that I am "clear to travel." *Is anyone really in charge here?* Two hours later, I finally escape all the security measures and call Jerry and Emmanuel to see if they're still waiting for me in the parking lot. To my relief they answer, "Yes, brother, we're outside waiting." *Praise God.*

As I exit the gate, my two brothers run toward me and embrace me in a hug so tight that it knocks the wind out of me. "What was taking you so long to come outside? You had us worried there," they say between joyful laughs.

"I thought I'd never get out," I jokingly confess as they release their grip on me and I breathe in the warm Liberian air. *I could kiss the ground right now.* Like old times, we hop in Jerry's dilapidated car and make our way toward the city of Monrovia.

Jerry's car hasn't had many improvements since the last time I was here. In fact, it now has only one functioning headlight that barely cuts the night as we bump down this dark road with no streetlights. I'm the only one who buckles into a seat belt. My American worry kicks in while my Liberian brothers remain cool as cucumbers.

It's a sheer miracle, but we pull into the Royal Grand Hotel safely. However, because of our late arrival, the entry gates have already been closed. *Oh, heck no. My family will not sleep on the street tonight!* My brothers and I beat on the gate as hard and loud as we can until a guard on duty convinces the concierge to let us through. We park, and I check in for my hotel room. *One hundred and fifty dollars a night!? I thought the prices here would be cheaper?* I sense they may be taking advantage of me, but I pay anyway because this is a nice hotel and I'm ready to just be settled.

As my brothers help me carry my stuff into the room, I ask if they'd like to come with me to see my mom. "Of course, Cammué. It's only a fifteen-minute walk," they reply.

"I'm great with walking. Let's go see my O'ma!" I cheer.

As we "count light poles" (a Liberian saying for "walking for an extended period of time"), I'm taken back to when I used to roam these same streets as a boy. We would always run in between cars while trying to cross the street, hoping we wouldn't get hit. (There are crosswalks and sidewalks now, but there were none back then.) We'd sell plastic bags to shoppers in the market and ice-cold water and Kool-Aid at the junction where all the cabmen would stop to pick up passengers.

Here, with my brothers, I am Cammué again. And I'm alive.

As we walk the streets, my brothers warn me to conceal my iPhone or anything nice. I've been walking around like I'm in the US. The reality check reminds me that I'm not in the suburbs of Charlotte anymore. Here, we could get robbed easily. I tuck everything out of sight as we approach the compound where my family is waiting. I've rented this apartment ahead of time, so they will all have a place to stay near my hotel. I can't believe I'm about to see my mom in real life!

Mom

The door opens and there she is: my mom. She has aged some, but she still looks the same as I remember her—raw-cocoa-colored skin; smart, kind eyes; and a small but strong stature. She's sitting in a chair when our eyes connect. With her hair tied back in a bandana, I can see every inch of her smile that so clearly spreads across her face as she wraps me in a warm hug. Our embrace is full of gratitude, and yet there's a note of mourning hanging over the moment because we are also holding the weight of all the years that have passed between us. All the time that was stolen from us, time we will never get back.

The rest of the family follows in a grand group embrace as they laugh and let happy tears flow freely. As the center of the pile, I can feel loved ones leaving the hug one by one, allowing in the smell of Liberian food. Mom finally lets me go as I'm handed a steaming, fragrant bowl of fufu and pepper soup* with chicken.

I wash my hands because, for this meal, I'm not going to use a spoon. As if we're in the village, I'm going to dig in with my hands. I go in for my first bite and hear, "It's so good to see you, big brother." My younger brother, Emmanuel, walks over and declares proudly, "That chicken you're eating was raised by me since it was just a chick. I prepared this just for you."

Just for me? Wow. I'm overwhelmed that someone who has barely seen me and knows so little about me would sacrifice that much on my behalf. Their animal. Time. Preparation. I've only been here a few hours, and I'm so moved.

Chicken, oddly enough, has seemed to be a connecting factor in my life. My first meal in America was KFC. I went on to be adopted by a man who owned Chick-fil-As. I worked for Chick-fil-A and went on to do their Impact 360 program. While chicken has blessed my life in so many ways at this point, none of that compares to the way my brother cared for, prepared, and served this chicken to me now as a symbol of love. Now THIS is some "Jesus chicken."

As I fill my stomach with fufu, the part of my heart that felt so empty begins to feel full again too.

Time fast-forwards and now it is morning at the hotel. My mom is sitting in the lobby waiting when I enter.

"Mom, what are you doing awake so early?" I ask as I greet her in the lobby.

"I just want to hang out, talk, and watch TV together," she replies.

The hotel serves a complimentary breakfast, so my mom, my brothers, and I take full advantage of the Liberian delicacies. We fill our plates with plantains, yams, cassava, eggs, and bacon … and then we go up to my room.

Mom sits down on my bed, crosses her feet, and reclines back. We relax all morning. Our history seems less complex as we lean into this simple, normal moment. Together.

Scenes from the following events roll by in slow motion with happy music playing in the background as I narrate.

While I didn't have much money in America, what I do have could make a difference for my family in Liberia. They may never get the wild experiences I was given—coming to the US, shopping at Goodwill, or eating from a buffet. So I do what I can to recreate that for them. I treat everyone to lunch one afternoon, take my mom and sisters shopping for a few things in the market, and surprise everyone with gifts of clothes, watches, and shoes from my suitcases. My dad still serves as a leader in his village, so I give him a briefcase shoulder bag to carry his paperwork. Oh, the joy I feel watching everyone try on their new accessories and outfits! What they lack in provision, I have been lacking in community and belonging. Really, we all meet each other's needs throughout the week, giving what we have to offer. But there's still one thing I really need before I head back to the States, something that only my Liberian mom can give me: peace of mind.

Music shifts to something a little more serious.

One evening after having family dinner, I sit down with my mom to have a conversation regarding the topic that's been top of my mind. I confess to her how stressed Amanda and I have been through several years of infertility. It feels like a silly question, but it's been burning in my mind for years. I have to have an answer. So I dare to ask, "Is someone in the family playing witchcraft on Amanda and me?"

"No, son. I am your mother. I'm the only one who God has given power over you," she replies with authority. "No one can play witchcraft or curse you besides me."

Despite being a grown man, I'm hit with overwhelming relief because I'm still a son who needs affirmation from his mother. And that's exactly what she's given me.

Tears roll down my cheeks as Mom stands, holds out her hands, and asks me to kneel before her while she blesses me in our native language. Immediately, because of the power of my mother's heartfelt prayer, my hopelessness shifts to hope.

I'd started this journey thinking our family may be cursed, but now in this moment, I am certain we are blessed.

I came here feeling lonely, and now I'm with my village.

I arrived feeling hopeless, and now I'm hopeful for the future God has planned for me.

It feels as if our entire family legacy shifts in this moment, and I promise God that if He will allow me to become a father, I will pass on the power of giving my own blessing for my children. Like Numbers 6:24–26 proclaims, I will speak over them, "The LORD bless you and keep you; the LORD make His face shine upon you, and be gracious to you. The LORD lift up His countenance upon you, and give you peace" (NKJV).

May we have children. May they be blessed. Amen.

Music fades out and scene cuts to Jackson sitting on a stool telling the following story.

If you traveled during the Coronavirus epidemic, you may remember that it was not for the faint of heart. Each government had established strict protocols with hopes of reducing casualties around the world.

One of the requirements for flying out of Liberia is that you have to test negative for Covid before departure (just as I did upon arrival).

My little brother, Emmanuel, has not left my side during this trip. He has been staying with me at the hotel, where he wakes up early every day to grab us breakfast, and he even offers to carry my bags for me whenever we venture out. He won't let me out of his sight. So of course he accompanies me to the clinic to take my Covid test.

At the clinic, we wait in line for three hours only to have to wait even longer back at the hotel for a phone call with my results. When the phone finally rings, I answer.

"Jackson TerKeurst?" the employee asks.

"Yup," I confirm, hoping he'll cut to the chase. I'm missing Amanda so much at this point and desperately want to pass the test so I can get back home to my wife.

"I'm sorry to tell you that your test result came back positive," he delivers the blow.

"How? I'm not sick. I don't even have any symptoms!" I reply in disbelief.

The employee huffs on the line as if he's frustrated that he's heard this response a hundred times today. "Sir," he continues, "you will need to isolate yourself in quarantine for five more days before we can send a medical person to come back to check on you. Based on their observation of your case, they will decide whether you are well enough to retake the test or need to stay isolated."

I slam the phone down without saying goodbye. I am heated. My flight is scheduled to leave in 72 hours, and they are telling me that I have to wait an additional week—or maybe longer—before I can go back home! I don't have the budget for that. Amanda and I are so low on cash at this point because of IVF expenses (and paying off our student loans). I have already spent everything I could on this trip. What will I do?

Immediately, I call Amanda and give her the bad news. She is just as mad as I am.

Finally, I get in touch with a very close friend who agrees to loan us the money so I can find a place to stay here for a few more weeks. It's awkward and, truthfully, a bit embarrassing to have to ask for money like this. I try to find the bright side.

After being stuck in a hotel for an entire week, I finally find out that the only thing the employees wanted was my money. My brother Emmanuel tells me that if I can give these guys cash, they will be more than happy to reverse the falsified Covid results. This is the best news I have ever heard. I can't wait to break out of the jail, I mean … hotel.

The next morning, we drive back to the health clinic where I pay a guy one hundred US dollars to get me the negative result that I need. Of course, it costs a ton of money to switch flights, but one "negative Covid test" and a few days later, I'm finally allowed to board the plane and head home.

Life lesson: Always purchase travel insurance.

Scene change.

Lights up and it's today, as you're reading this book. I'm sitting across from you at a Starbucks. You're holding your favorite beverage. I'm sipping my venti iced coffee with classic syrup and half cream while I get to tell you this exciting news.

I'm in the process of rebuilding my mother's house, the one that was burned to the ground by rebels in the opening chapter. Yes! That house! The one I fled with my aunt before finding refuge in the jungle.

I can't believe it either. Our story is coming full circle.

Let me tell you about it. My mom's new house will be the only "civilized" concrete house in our village. Initially, my family was able to rebuild some of her house with clay bricks. Cement is very expensive in Liberia, so most of us still use mud from the creek to mold into blocks. But now I get to help my mom rebuild her house with stable materials that will last. One day, I want to be able to save up enough to build an even better house so my mom can have her own bedroom and a comfortable mattress to lay her head on at night.

Hey, look at all God has provided for us. I believe He'll do it again! Don't you?

End scene.

Scene 2: Where Is the TerKeurst Tribe Now?

Lights up on Amanda and me. We're in our apartment. It's 2023, and we're sitting on the couch resting. Amanda's phone sits on the coffee table, and we hover over it like flies drawn to the blue light.

Amanda and I have both been at work all day and are now anxiously awaiting the call about the results of our pregnancy test. We have been trying different IVF treatments for more than six and a half years. This is the fifth time we have waited on a call like this, and we're hoping that, this time, we won't be hanging up in heartache.

The phone notifies us that there's a new voicemail, and we scoot close together on the couch as Amanda hits play. "Hello!" Detecting a tinge of happiness in the nurse's tone, my spirits start to soar. "I'm so excited to be calling you with positive news. Your test today did come back positive. Everything looks fantastic!"

Amanda is sobbing true tears of joy, and I sit with my eyes wide and mouth gaping open in shock. *So this is what it's like when you receive a miracle.* Finally, we scream, embrace, and participate in a long-awaited celebration. We're finally going to be parents!

We listen to that voicemail at least four more times. It only seems to get better, sweeter each time we hear the news.

Time fast-forwards. I'm on the couch with a laptop in my lap typing away, working on this book, as Amanda walks through the door.

Amanda comes home from another lab draw, and her numbers have more than doubled. This means we aren't just having one baby. We're having two! A baby girl and boy at that! Our heart and our legacy. Thank You, God!

Praise Jehovah-Jireh, God the provider. Praise El Roi, the God who sees.

> God is who He says He is.
> I am who He says I am.
> I'm Jackson AND I'm Cammué. And I'm going to
> be a dad!
> So I keep moving forward.

End scene.

Scene 3: The Interview

A black backdrop hangs behind me. I'm sitting in a simple chair being interviewed by you, the show's host.

"Now that you've told your story, who are you? How did looking back help you go forward?" you ask.

"Well," I start confidently. "Telling you about my past set me free to keep moving forward into becoming ... me.

"Looking back, I discovered that 'me' is who I have always been. Just like you have always been you.

"You see, we're not defined by our past. But we *are* the sum of all our former experiences. While our sins are forgiven in Christ—as well as all the transgressions committed against us—the lessons are never forgotten. It's there at the center of who we were and who God is allowing us to become that we discover who we are—the beloved child of God who was (and forever will be) 'me.'

"We must look back, outside of time, space, and circumstance, to discover that there, in the very middle of it all, Jesus has always held the center. He has always been there in my life, your life, all of history, the past, present, and future. Jesus is there, mending our broken stories and empowering us to turn another page or start another chapter in life.

"Looking back, I can see that every version of me was not a surprise to God because my life was already written by His Word."

Cut to a clip of a younger version of Jackson appearing on the screen. He's an orphan around twelve years old dressed in worn clothing with no shoes. He's smiling and running down the Liberian shore toward the camera like a kid playing a game with his friends on an African beach. My voice narrates over the clip.

"Psalm 113:7–9 says, 'He raises the poor from the dust and lifts the needy from the ash heap ...'"

All of a sudden, in front of twelve-year-old Jackson appears twenty-two-year-old Jackson. The younger Jackson keeps running forward, until he crashes straight into the older Jackson and disappears. Twenty-two-year-old Jackson wears

American clothes and looks like a college kid. He has a book bag draped over his shoulder and seems to be chatting with friends offscreen. He casually walks forward, as if he's strolling to class across his college campus. My voice continues ...

"... he seats them with princes, with the princes of his people...."

I am twenty-two-year-old Jackson. I enter a hospital, where thirty-five-year-old Jackson appears. He's standing over two bassinets with tears streaming down his face. He bends down carefully and picks up two babies, each swaddled cozily in his arms. Based on the pink and blue hats, he holds one baby boy and one baby girl. Carrying his children like treasures, this older Jackson begins to walk toward me. I make eye contact with this proud new father, nod my head in a knowing manner, and quote this portion of the Bible verse to him ...

"... He settles the childless woman in her home as a happy mother of children...."

As thirty-five-year-old Jackson appears now with the babies, he smiles and puts the babies into my arms. He then disappears, as I look straight into the camera with joy-filled tears spilling from my eyes. I conclude the verse ...

"... Praise the LORD!"

The screen goes black. End scene.

Who was I?

I was the …
Grandson of a witch doctor.
The son of a town chief.
A Liberian orphan.
A statistic of war.
Nameless.
Homeless.
Barely alive.

Now, I am:

Called by name.
Adopted.
Chosen.
Married.
Loved.
Home.
Fully alive.

So, who am I?

I'm who I was, am, and am becoming.
I'm Cammué Gweh.

I'm Jackson TerKeurst.

Now that I've gone back, I can keep moving forward, trusting the God who has brought me
this far and continues to carry me through.

So, now for the bigger question:

Who are you?

AFTERWORD

from Kaley

When Jackson asked me to help him write this book, I was stunned. *Me? You want me to help tell your story?*

I instantly knew this was something only God could orchestrate. It was with the greatest honor and excitement that I began to dive into Jackson's past, present, and hope for the future.

Telling the story of a war orphan is not an easy task. As a mom with three children of my own, I cried more tears than I could count listening to Jackson recount his memories. I gave my best shot at helping him put words to these graphic and heart-wrenching moments. Yet, through even the darkest parts of Jackson's story, there was always a glimmer catching my mind's eye—openings where God's light was so evidently shining through.

My hope is that those rays of light shine bright in your soul and pierce your heart just as they have mine. I pray you feel inspired to know *your* true identity in Christ and to claim the home and family you have with Him, no matter where life may take you.

My overarching dream is that, because of this book, orphans will be adopted, cultural perspectives and barriers will be broken down, the lost will find a home, and we will all be reinvigorated by looking at our own pasts to find a future hope in the God who brings us all into His family.

Thank you for reading *The Only Way Forward Is Back*. Now, go change the world.

For His glory,
Kaley

ACKNOWLEDGMENTS

I would like to start out by thanking God for using me as an instrument to reach others with the incredible testimony He has given me. There are not enough words to convey my gratitude to Him for providing for me and protecting me even in the most chaotic circumstances. I want to pour out my thanks to Him for always keeping His promises and revealing His plans for my life.

To my Liberian O'ma (Keyneh) and Papay (D. Henson Gweh), thank you for the fond memories we shared as a family unit growing up in Africa. You both always pushed and inspired me to pursue education as a poor boy. Now that I understand why, I would like to extend to you both my gratitude for making one of the toughest decisions of your lives, to give up your son so he could find safety and life in the most dire of circumstances.

Pastor Kofi and the ACFI ministry team, you all are my physical and spiritual superheroes. I cannot thank you enough for your incredible heart for God and all His children. You allowed God to use you in a very unique and special way to spread His Word and compassion for those in need. I will forever be grateful to you, Pastor Kofi, and your family for taking me into your home, protecting me, providing for me, teaching me about Jesus, and teaching me life's greatest lessons and principles. Thank you to all the caregivers at each of the orphanages I lived in. I am alive because of your nurturing hearts, kind spirits, and motherly love, and I will forever be grateful that you chose to love me and care for me as your own. Not to mention how you woke up each and every morning, went to the well to draw water, and started a fire out of nothing just so I could have warm water for a bath before school. You taught me how to wash and iron my own clothes, and how to hang them on a rope for the warm ocean breeze to dry them. You taught me the importance of waking up early, making my bed, and having devotions each morning. I thank you for the unlimited and consistent days you went above and beyond to prep big pots of rice and beans so I could have food in my belly (when it was available). You all saved my life.

To my brothers in song, growing up together in the orphanage, we may not have had much, but we had each other. Through music and laughter, we found strength in the hardest of times. Our voices rose above our struggles, and our bond became unbreakable. We were more than just a choir—we were a family. Though life has taken us in different directions, the memories we created and the love we shared will always remain. No matter where we are in the world, we will always be connected by the melodies we sang, the laughter we shared, and the unshakable bond we built. I am forever grateful for each of you. We are, and always will be, brothers.

To my mom and dad (Lysa and Art), thank you for listening to God and trusting Him to make possible the impossible. You accepted me as a son, provided for me in every way, and displayed at home what godly leaders are. You both taught me lessons that I will cherish and hold on to for the rest of my life. I wouldn't be anywhere close to where I am today without you.

Ashley, Hope, and Brooke, thank you all for opening your hearts to allow God to use you in such a special way. From the first day we all met in the pews of that church and chased each other like siblings, I felt connected to you for life. Thank you for choosing Liberia as a country to do for your Girl Scout project. What a wild thing! I love you all to pieces and will still always break someone for you if they ever think of harming you in any way. You have a big brother in me as long as I'm alive and breathing. Believe that!

Mark, you're my best friend turned brother. There isn't any way I can really put that into words. But I'm so grateful God chose us to stand side by side.

Amanda, thank you for loving me unconditionally on a daily basis and for blessing me with our beautiful children, Legend and Londyn. We've birthed two babies and a book! Who would have dreamed? I love how courageous you are, and I admire how much you love others and Jesus. You are truly my biggest inspiration. (And you'll always be "The One.")

Legend and Londyn, I dedicate this memoir to you. I hope our story inspires you to set your standards high and choose the path in life that many choose not to take. You are my greatest joy and blessings. Words cannot describe the level of happiness you bring into our lives. I want you to remember that Mommy and Daddy love you very much and will always be here for you as long as God lets us. I encourage you to always be yourself, to trust God and His plan for your life, and to stay true to yourself despite what the world throws at you. Treat everyone you meet with honor, dignity, and respect. And don't forget to always create fun wherever you go!

Darin Short, thank you for lending us your expertise on trauma and counseling. You offered us access to information we never even knew existed, and we hope these tools will encourage many children and families for years to come.

To my friends who have been there from day one (you know who you are), I appreciate you walking beside me through thick and thin. I am grateful that God brought each of you into my life. You have played a major role in my development, and you've helped me understand the world for what it is. I hope our friendships last a lifetime.

Austin, Kaley, and the David C Cook Team, I cannot express how grateful I am that God brought you all my way. I prayed for years that God would send me someone who would believe in me, believe in my story. He sent me an angel named Kaley, and then Austin, and now the team at David C Cook who have given me the opportunity of a lifetime. You all believed in me when other publishing houses and writers did not. Thank you from the bottom of my heart for seeing what God is trying to do with the incredible testimony He has given me. I am astonished that He chose us to spread this beautiful message to all His children.

Sincerely,

Jackson

LIBERIAN DICTIONARY

Words used in this book that are best defined through Liberian context and in Jackson's own words are marked with an asterisk (*).

Auntie—A term referring to an aunt or other adult woman who is considered a very close, respected, and loved family member or friend.

Cammué—I'm named after my paternal great-grandfather and grandfather. Cammué is a generational name meaning "Little Giant" in the Kpelle tribal language.

Cassava—A root vegetable, this is one of the most staple foods eaten on a daily basis in Liberia. Once the roots are ready to harvest off the cassava plant, some will surface from the ground or create a crack in the ground. They are then dug up and prepared.

Dashiki—Traditional West African Lappa suit made up of a loose, brightly colored or embroidered tunic. The Mothers in the orphanage wore this with skirts because, at the time, it was improper for women to wear pants. They wore the entire set from head to toe with slippers. These outfits were considered their best garments.

Fufu and pepper soup—Fufu is traditional West African cuisine and the top swallow (dough-based African staples made of vegetables or grains) food. It is made from plantains, yams, and/or cassava roots and is typically prepared by mixing it with water and beating it into a dough-like paste. Pepper soup is a simple soup typically consisting of a choice of meat or protein. I typically prepare mine with fish, okra, and benne seeds.

Ganga ball—A tennis-like ball made from rubber trees. It is very bouncy. We used this as a form of football (soccer in America) since we couldn't afford the actual ball. Growing up in the village, my family owned a rubber plantation. We planted these trees when they were just seeds. Once grown to the appropriate size, we would slice different parts of the trees to produce the liquid that we then molded together to form a ganga ball.

Gbarnga—The capital city of Bong County, which lies northeast of Monrovia. This city belongs to the Kpelle tribe, which is my family tribe.

Koloqua—Derived from Liberian interior pidgin English and known as Liberian Kreyol, this is a special dialectic spoken widely by Liberian natives.

Lappa—A childhood game played with two teams (typically boys against girls). Prior to the start, all the players mix their slippers, shoes, and sandals in a pile. One player from team A gets in the middle and tries to get all the pairs in proper order. The opposing team's players throw a ganga ball (see above) to knock out the player in the middle before he or she can pair up the shoes. If all players on team A are knocked out by the pitchers, then it becomes team B's turn to correctly sort the shoes.

Mother—Similar to "O'ma" or "Oldma." A term of endearment for caregivers or women at the orphanage. Someone in position of providing nurture and care to children.

Nae Keyneh—Nae (meaning mother). Mother Keyneh.

O'ma—A name often used when referring to our mother. It is also an endearing term used as a sign of love and respect for other women we admire who may not be in our biological family. It is also often spelled as "oldma."

Papay—How my siblings and I referred to our father growing up in the village. It is also a term of endearment for a male figure who is older than us.

Pekin—A term of endearment used when referring to a younger child (specifically boys) or brother.

Rooted ropes—Indigenous roots found in the jungle that we used to tie bamboo canes together to make temporary rafts. Various kinds of rooted ropes can be found in Liberia's rainforests or jungles.

Sasa—A percussion instrument made from a gourd. The player holds the long, pointed end. The round part of the gourd is covered with strings entangled with beads. The player shakes and rubs the instrument to make distinctive sounds. It's typically used during church ceremonies or rituals.

Shekere cup—Said to hold the water to life, this is the meaning of my last name "Gweh."

HOW TO SUPPORT ACFI

African Christians Fellowship International (ACFI) is the organization you read the most about in this book. It was through ACFI that Jackson was nourished back to life and brought to America. It's still a thriving organization with a stateside base in Lancaster, South Carolina. You can be a part of furthering their mission to change the lives of orphans like Jackson.

Background

ACFI was founded by Edward (Pastor Kofi) and Cecelia Kofi in 1989 to reach the people in rural Liberia and the subregion of West Africa with the gospel message. During the fourteen-year Liberian Civil War (1989–2004), their mission expanded to include humanitarian aid as they established orphanages and provided medical assistance to those in need. They continue to serve in all these areas.

Their Mission

1. Be a light in a dark world.
2. Serve via medical clinics, agricultural development, and relief ministry.
3. Make disciples and spread the gospel.

4. Strengthen the body of Christ through
   pastor training, evangelistic outreach,
   and the Christian college program.

You can help support ACFI by donating directly to their program, volunteering for a short- or long-term mission trip, writing letters to children and pastors, praying, or sponsoring a child.

Jump in and get involved by visiting their website at www.acfiliberia.info.

NOTES

Section 1: Foblite Is on Fire

1. Samuel Momodu, "First Liberian Civil War (1989–1996)," Black Past, July 25, 2016, www.blackpast.org/global-african-history/first-liberian-civil-war-1989-1996.

2. "Liberia Country Profile," BBC News, February 13, 2024, www.bbc.com /news/world-africa-13729504.

3. John H. Thomson, "The Liberian Coup D'Etat: Its Impact on Economic and Security Assistance" (study project, US Army War College, 1988) 37, https:// apps.dtic.mil/sti/tr/pdf/ADA195745.pdf.

4. Charles Rivers Editors, *The End of Democracy in Liberia: The History of the Coups That Overthrew Liberia's Leaders in the 1980s and Led to Civil War*, CreateSpace Independent Publishing Platform, 2018.

5. T. Christian Miller, "Firestone and the Warlord: Warlord on the Rise," ProPublica, November 18, 2014, www.propublica.org/article/firestone-and -the-warlord-chapter-1.

6. Charles Rivers Editors, *The End of Democracy in Liberia*, CreateSpace.

Section 2: Trusting God in Abandonment

1. William Shakespeare, *Romeo and Juliet*, Act II, Scene II, essay, Harrap's (2021).

2. Joe Taysom, ed., "The Heartfelt Letter Louis Armstrong Wrote to a Fan: 'Music Is Life Itself,'" *Far Out Magazine*, August 4, 2020, https://faroutmagazine.co.uk /heartfelt-letter-louis-armstrong-wrote-to-fan.

Section 4: An Orphan Finds a Home

1. "Lysa Terkeurst," Proverbs 31 Ministries Speakers, 2023, proverbs31.org /speakers/lysa-terkeurst.

2. Allison Torres Burtka, "Scarcity Mentality: Causes, Symptoms, and More," WebMD, October 2, 2024, www.webmd.com/mental-health/what-is-scarcity-mentality.

Section 5: Listen and Learn
1. Rebecca Ruiz, "Community Adopts 45 Orphans from War-Torn Country," *Today*, May 30, 2013, www.today.com/news/community-adopts-45-orphans-war-torn-country-6c10109865.

Section 6: Family
1. "Divorce Statistics for 2022," Petrelli Previtera LLC, accessed February 13, 2024, www.petrellilaw.com/divorce-statistics-for-2022.

Section 7: How to Look Back to Go Forward
1. "The Power of Sankofa: Know History," Berea College, accessed April 17, 2023, www.berea.edu/centers/carter-g-woodson-center-for-interracial-education/the-power-of-sankofa#.

2. "Lesson 6: Don't Forget Who You Belong To," Biblical Stewardship Resource Library, accessed February 13, 2024, stewardshiplibrary.com/lesson-6-dont-forget-who-you-belong-to.

3. *Frozen II*, directed by Chris Buck and Jennifer Lee (Walt Disney Studios Home Entertainment: Burbank, CA, 2019).

4. Adam Young, "The Big Six," Adam Young Counseling, accessed February 28, 2023, adamyoungcounseling.com/free-documents.

5. Kelsie Goller, "Choices, Cookies, and Kids: A Class Garry Landreth Training," Kranz Psychological Services, accessed July 12, 2023, www.kranzpsychservices.com/single-post/cookies-choices-and-kids-a-class-garry-landreth-training.